First published in 2009 by Voyageur Press, an imprint of MBI Publishing Company,
400 First Avenue North, Suite 300, Minneapolis, MN 55401 USA

Voyageur Press titles are also available at discounts in bulk quantity for industrial or
sales-promotional use. For details write to Special Sales Manager at MBI Publishing Company,
400 First Avenue North, Suite 300, Minneapolis, MN 55401 USA.

To find out more about our books, visit us online at www.voyageurpress.com.

ISBN-13: 978-0-7603-3525-3

Editor: Kari Cornell
Series design: Lois Stanfield
Layout design: Cindy Samargia Laun

Printed in China

Library of Congress Cataloging-in-Publication Data

The farmer's wife canning and preserving cookbook : over 250 blue-ribbon recipes! /
    Lela Nargi, editor. — 1st ed.
    p. cm.
Includes bibliographical references and index.
ISBN 978-0-7603-3525-3 (comb : alk. paper)
    1. Canning and preserving. I. Nargi, Lela. II. Farmer's wife magazine.
TX603.F368 2009
641.4--dc22
2008041422

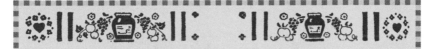

The Farmer's Wife Canning and Preserving Cookbook

OVER 250 BLUE-RIBBON RECIPES

LELA NARGI, EDITOR

Voyageur Press

Contents

You CAN Can

Introduction

The *Farmer's Wife* was a monthly magazine published in Minnesota between the years 1893 and 1939. In an era long before the Internet and high-speed travel connected us all, the magazine aimed to offer community among hard-working rural women: to provide a forum for their questions and concerns and to assist them in the day-to-day goings-on about the farm—everything from raising chickens and slaughtering hogs to managing scant funds, dressing the children, keeping house, and running the kitchen.

Decades before the advent of *Cook's Illustrated* and its monthly doses of kitchen science, there was *The Farmer's Wife* and its own science-based methodology, culled from staff experts, bulletins issued by the U.S. Department of Agriculture (USDA), and various extension services across the country. On no kitchen topic was the magazine's expertise more critical than on preserving. Preserving then required—and most assuredly still does—precise procedures in order to yield wholesome, safe foodstuffs. A farmer's wife had plenty to preserve. She put up myriad stores from her gardens, fields, and orchards—not just the niceties of jams and jellies and pickles but the fundamentals of plain fruits, vegetables, sauces, and soups that formed the backbone of meals during the long, cold months when nothing grew.

Come March, the magazine was chockfull of articles on what to plant to ensure large and diverse crops for end-of-summer canning.

Come May, articles abounded on community canning clubs (as if
it weren't enough that a farmer's wife preserved food for her own
family's needs, she and her daughters often made extra money by
canning all manner of garden bounty to sell at county fairs, local
stores, and to city women with no gardens of their own). June marked
the beginning of a four-month flurry of recipes, news of updates in
processing procedures, and the latest must-have gadgets, tips for
achieving crisp pickles and pert jellies, and on and on and on. Even
in December *The Farmer's Wife* offered recipes for canning citrus and
tropical fruits shipped in from distant regions and for cooking up
what was already in the cans.

Nothing would have signified a greater failure of farmer's
wifery than a scantly-stocked canning cupboard. Unbountiful
stores would have indicated a failure of crop raising, or a failure of
thrift, or a failure of time-management (or, most horrifying of all,
a failure of all three!), resulting in a winning-out of the greatest of
all sins: sloth. Presented here in this book are some 250 recipes and
procedures culled from the pages of *The Farmer's Wife*. Contemporary
canning enthusiasts may experience for themselves the delightfully
industrious stockpiling that made the farmer's wife prepared for
just about anything, but most of all, for winter. The recipes will
appeal not only to country gardeners who cringe at the thought of
home-grown bounty gone to waste but also to urban farmers' market-
goers who would find a way to extend a little bucolic cheer into an
otherwise fruit-less environment.

Canning methods have changed significantly since the days of
The Farmer's Wife and even over the course of the past ten years,
so be sure to read the "Read This First" section of this book before
proceeding, as well as the "The Basics" section at the beginning of
each chapter. There is a lot of valuable, ever-updating information on
preserving available to home canners, so also be certain to consult
the additional resources list at the end of this book. And now, get
ready to roll up your sleeves and knuckle down to the delights of *The
Farmer's Wife*'s canning and pickling kitchen!

YOURS FOR EASIER CANNING

By Ina B. Rowe
June 1937

In our mind's eye and with a pair of imaginary scissors, let's snip a dollar into small change, and let it flutter piecemeal to those special gadgets which lessen canning labor. Some of those suggested may be bought for a nickel or a dime. Some may cost as much as a quarter.

First on our list is a brush for jars, especially the old ones. Since canning success depends on cleanliness from start to finish, we must start with a jar well scrubbed with sudsy water inside and out. A fine mesh metal dishcloth is a help around the shoulder of any jar, and particularly around the screw threads of a Mason closure.

And while we are on the subject of scrubbing, jars respond best to washing either in soft water, hard water well broken with a softener, or with one of the soap-like substances that leaves no gummy residue. The reason? Spoilage bacteria gain an easy foothold on a sticky surface.

Since an extra pair of hands cannot always be had for the asking, an extra handler to lift and lower jars is a big help. Some jar lifters tighten on the shoulder when you grip the handle. Others are double jointed and let go under pressure. Either does the work if you know when to grip. Otherwise it may let you down at a crucial moment. Choose one that seems to cooperate well, and try to find one with enough reach to take hold of a wide mouth jar.

When glass is put into boiling water to process, breakage is less if you let go quickly. Do not dangle the lower rim in the boiling water while making up your mind where it is going to land. It is like taking a cold plunge in late October. The temperature is less startling if you take it with a quick jump. A metal rack is best because it sinks, and the jars go into the water quickly. So perhaps a few cents of the dollar will go to the hardware dealer for a square of half- or quarter-inch screen.

Rubber wrenches to fit the tops of narrow-gauge Masons protect your hands from the heat of the jar. However, do not let any wrench persuade you to think that a screw-cap closure calls for great strength of hand. "Snug" is tight enough. The vacuum forming within the jar as it cools is what creates the seal.

An aluminum cup with a wooden handle cannot do a high dive to the bottom of a full kettle, and the handle will remain comparatively cool. Shop around for the right one. Some measuring cups are made of such lightweight metal that when empty, they tip. This may not annoy you, but it is a great trial to me.

We cannot supply asbestos fingers, but we have something just as good. For example, rubber pads which are waterproof and also proof against the steam burns so often suffered when a hot jar is gripped with a damp towel. Rubber gloves are a big help, too, both because they protect the fingers from hot food, and also because they protect the food from never-too-sanitary fingers.

Our slogan: every jar a wide mouth jar! We widen narrow tops by means of the fruit funnel. Small fry, like peas, beans, and corn, slip in easily even when our aim is very poor.

Our favorite labeling gadget is a colored pencil—not the kind you take from little Junior's school kit, but a regular china marking pencil made for writing on glass. It works best when the glass is warm but not hot. In jelly-making season, label *Strawb. 1937* with a yellow pencil and green *Mint* with a red pencil, so that the writing will show against the color of the food.

Here is one for you and your handyman to make. It is a pusher for crowding whole tomatoes down into the jars so as to squeeze out the air and bring up juice to cover. It is made like the dasher of a churn, a perforated disk to fit into the jar, mounted on a handle, long and strong, so that we dare to use plenty of push.

Read This First: How to Get Started

S ome 250 recipes and procedures for preserving a variety of fruits and vegetables, in a whole host of ways, appear in this book. To ensure success and safety in preserving them, it is important to understand a bit about how preserving works and why.

Some of the preserved foods in this book, such as jams, jellies, and other sweet spreads, lend themselves to preservation because they are made up of high-acid foods (fruits) cooked with high concentrations of sugar. Some of them, such as chutneys and certain pickles, are combinations of high-acid and low-acid foods (which include meats, all vegetables, and sometimes tomatoes) that are preserved by precise additions of sugar, salt, and/or vinegar. Still others—fruits and vegetables canned without sugar, salt, or vinegar—are rendered free of potential toxins and therefore safe to eat by processing for prescribed periods of time at high temperatures.

In fact, these days, unlike during the era of *The Farmer's Wife*, it is recommended that *all* canned foods be processed after packing in jars to eliminate any risk of contamination with molds and bacteria. There are two ways to do this, and nowadays, they are the *only* ways recommended by the U.S. Department of Agriculture (USDA) and food safety experts:

The *boiling water bath*, in which jars of food are immersed in water in a boiling water canner or large stockpot and the water brought to a boil for a prescribed time, and the *pressure canner*, which heats water to a number of degrees above boiling. These two methods are not created equal, and it is important to be aware of the differences between them and when it is appropriate to use one or the other.

A *note about sterilizing and processing times given in this book:* They are for altitudes of 0 to 1,000 feet *only*. If you live at an altitude above 1,000 feet, you *must* consult one of the sources listed at the end of this book or your local extension service to ascertain the correct processing time for your altitude. Failure to make adjustments for altitude will result in products that are potentially unsafe to eat.

The boiling water bath, as indicated by its name, processes food at the temperature of boiling water. It is recommended *only* for high-acid foods, which include all fruit products, all pickled products, and sometimes, tomatoes. The tomato, once considered a high-acid food, is now known to be inconsistent in its acidity levels. This is why it is recommended that lemon juice be added to certain tomato products (this topic is covered in greater detail in the chapter titled "Preserved Tomatoes and Tomato Products").

The pressure canner processes foods at a higher temperature than the boiling water canner and is required for everything else: namely, all vegetables that are not pickled, anything that contains meat, poultry, or seafood, and sometimes, tomatoes.

In order to can fruit and vegetable products using either of these methods, you will need some specialized equipment and some other items that can readily be found around the house. These things vary a little depending on what you are canning, so consult the "The Basics" section in each chapter to make sure you have everything you need before getting started. All canning equipment must be

24-Quart Canner

Postpaid for only 2 three-year subscription orders for THE FARMER'S WIFE Magazine at $1 each... Reward No. 460G.
This big Water Bath Canner and Cooking Pot makes home canning easier and surer. Holds nine pint or seven quart jars. Special rack and instructions. Fine for whole hams or ear corn. Seamless blue enamelware.

Rotary Food Press

Postpaid for only 2 three-year subscription orders for THE FARMER'S WIFE Magazine at $1 each... Reward No. 414G.
Save hours of time and have finer pulp and juices. No peeling, no coring. Takes out skins and seeds. Presses, strains, rices, extracts and washes. Finest aluminum with sturdy frame and wooden roller. Non-overflow and self-cleaning. More from fruits and vegetables with less work.

Big 24-Qt. Preserving Kettle

Postpaid for only 2 three-year subscription orders for THE FARMER'S WIFE Magazine at $1 each... Reward No. 413G.
A big, new Preserving Kettle for canning and butchering time. Made of fine quality porcelain enamelware with a full capacity of twenty-four quarts—imagine the convenience when making jelly, canning fruit or rendering lard and how handy a really big kettle will be every so often.

Send your orders to
THE FARMER'S WIFE
St. Paul   *Magazine*   Minnesota

scrupulously clean and, in some instances, sterilized, so be sure you are clear about these methods (see page 21 for more information).

The USDA has published a set of guidelines that list methods and processing times for certain products. Invariably, these are products that have been tested by experts in land-grant universities. The methods and times should be followed exactly to minimize any risk of food-borne illness. For example, if a tested method for canning tomatoes calls for you to wash them, remove their cores, then plunge them in boiling water in order to remove their skins, this set of instructions is as critical to ensuring the safety of the tomatoes as the instructions that call for you to add a tablespoon of bottled lemon juice to each pint jar and for you to process the filled jars for forty minutes in a boiling water bath. Any deviation will result in a product that is potentially unsafe for long-term storage.

Every attempt has been made here to conform to these standards in all applicable recipes. If you have any questions whatsoever about a method or processing time, however, consult the USDA-supported website for the National Center for Home Food Preservation (NCHFP) (**www.uga.edu/nchfp**), the USDA's excellent "Complete Guide to Home Canning," which can be downloaded from this website, or contact a food safety expert at your

local cooperative extension service (**www.csrees .usda.gov/ Extension/**) will help you locate the extension service that is right for your area).

Obviously, it would take an untold number of centuries to test every canning recipe ever created, and certainly not every recipe that ever appeared in *The Farmer's Wife* has been tested for

safety. Nevertheless, many excellent and *untested* recipes have been included in this book. Pickles, relishes, chutneys, and other such products that have not yet been evaluated in a lab for safety can still be enjoyed for short-term use: that is, they may be cooked up, packed in jars, and stored in the refrigerator to be consumed within a week or two. These recipes appear in a gray box and are marked with a snowflake icon. Other recipes may be preserved by freezing. Only tested recipes should be canned. In this way, the myriad delicious recipes devised by *The Farmer's Wife* may continue to be enjoyed by contemporary cooks. The recipes are especially useful in cooking up small batches of produce from the home garden and farmers' market, when full canner loads would have been unfeasible to begin with.

Whatever your needs—for small or large batches of jams or jellies, pickles, or condiments—*The Farmer's Wife* offers something for everyone.

Sweet Spreads

Sweet spreads exist in abundance on the pages of *The Farmer's Wife*. They were and still are a wonderful way to treat fruit abundance from the garden and to insert a little summer sunshine into winter's gloom. Some sweet spreads are jellied, others (namely, the butters and honeys in this chapter) do not necessarily need to jell in order to be considered a success.

For the most part, *The Farmer's Wife* made jellied spreads without the use of commercial pectin, although a few recipes that use commercial pectin exist on the pages of the magazine. Some have been included here.

All methods and procedures in this chapter, except for untested, "refrigerator" recipes, have been checked for safety against the following sources: The NCHFP website, the Clemson University Extension Service website, and the University of Minnesota Extension Service website.

The Basics

Jellies are made by extracting juice from fruit then cooking the juice with sugar. They are clear, or translucent, and firm enough to hold their shape when they are turned out of the container.

Jams are thick, sweet spreads that are made by cooking crushed or chopped fruits with sugar. They hold their shape, too, but are usually less firm than jellies.

Conserves are jam-like spreads made from mixtures that may include citrus fruits, nuts, raisins, and coconut.

Marmalades are jellies that contain bits of fruit or peel. They are traditionally citrus, but other types of marmalades appear throughout the pages of the magazine.

Fruit butters and *honeys*, which are not jellied products, were also favored by *The Farmer's Wife* and are covered in this chapter. Fruit butters are a thick sort of fruit puree, and fruit honeys are a clear condiment with a drizzling consistency. Their treatment and processing are a bit different from jellied products, so pay close attention to variations in directions.

In order to jell properly, jellied spreads require high concentrations of pectin (which occurs naturally in fruit, to varying degrees; see chart on page 27), acid, and sugar. In order to make these spreads without the addition of commercial pectin, all these elements must exist in proper amounts. For this reason, it is recommended that at least one-quarter of the fruit used for these products be unripe (unripe fruit contains more pectin) and to be either of a high-pectin variety or a combination of high and low.

As you read on, you will notice that instructions for extracting juice and cooking it down recommend that you boil rapidly; this method is also intended to preserve pectin content, which breaks down at a simmer or slow boil. Sometimes it will be necessary to add lemon juice to jellies to raise their acid content.

To use all-ripe fruit or fruit of a low-pectin variety, commercial pectin must be added to the juice or fruit mixture, as directed by the individual manufacturer (directions vary with pectin brand and also between powdered and liquid types). From time to time, the farmer's wife certainly found herself with a quantity of ripe, end-of-season strawberries, for example, to cook into jam. For this reason, recipes calling for commercial pectin have not been dismissed out of hand for the purposes of this book. You should know, however, that commercial pectin products will be a far sight sweeter than those made without.

Once upon a time, it was deemed safe to preserve sweet spreads without processing them. This is no longer the case. All sweet spreads should be packed in sterilized half-pint jars and processed in a boiling water bath for five minutes (except for fruit butters and honeys, which may be packed in clean jars but then must be processed for fifteen minutes or according to specific instructions in each recipe). They must also be sealed with brand-new, two-piece lids; paraffin is no longer considered appropriate for sealing jars. These new recommendations discourage mold growth on sweet spreads.

Here is a list of the equipment you will need to make the recipes in this chapter:

■ Canning jars in half-pint sizes. Jars may be reused from one canning season to the next. However, you must make sure that they are in good shape, with no nicks or chips or signs of wear. Old or new, before using, they must be washed thoroughly in very hot water with soap or in the dish-washer. If the products they will hold are to  be processed for fewer than ten minutes (such as all the jellied spreads), they must also be sterilized, instructions for which appear on page 21. Jars with pop-top lids and any other sorts of jars are no longer recommended for use in home canning.

■ Two-part canning lids. These are available from grocery stores or canning supply stores and they are good for ONE USE ONLY. Follow the individual manufacturer's directions for cleaning and sterilizing to prepare the jars for use.

■ A boiling water canner or a large stock-pot. It should be deep enough to allow at least 1 to 2 inches of water to boil over the tops of the jars and have a rack to keep jars off the bottom.

■ An 8- or 10-quart saucepan for cooking fruit and juices. A larger pan is better, as jellies and jams have a tendency to boil over. A heavy metal pan is preferred because it allows for even heat distribution.

- A jelly bag, or a firm unbleached muslin or cotton flannel with the napped side turned in, or four thicknesses of closely woven cheesecloth, as well as a rack or colander for hanging. This is to extract juice from fruit after cooking. Dampen jelly bags or cloths before using them to extract the juice.

- Measuring cups and spoons.

- Stainless-steel cooking spoons.

- Large bowls for collecting juice.

- A jelly, candy, or deep-fat thermometer to determine doneness in sweet spreads that have no added commercial pectin.

- A jar lifter to remove hot jars from the canner.

- Clean dishtowels and paper towels for wiping jar rims and general cleanup.

- Timer or clock to determine the end of processing time.

- Dishtowels and racks for cooling jars after processing.

- A permanent marker for labeling the type of product and the date of its making on the jars.

Once you have assembled all this equipment and your ingredients, you are ready to begin. Follow these steps, as outlined on the NCHFP's website (**http://www.uga.edu/nchfp/publications/ uga/uga_processing_j_j.pdf**), before proceeding.

Note: All times, for sterilizing and processing, are for altitudes of between 0 and 1,000 feet. If you live at a higher altitude, additional times are necessary. Please consult your local extension agent for information about the sterilizing and processing times that are right for your area.

1. Wash half-pint canning jars in hot water with detergent and rinse well, or wash in the dishwasher. Sterilize by submerging 10 minutes in boiling water. (Butters and honeys, which will be processed for 15 minutes, can be packed into *clean* jars that have not been sterilized before use.) The easiest way to do this is to stand the empty jars upright on a rack in a boiling water canner filled with clean water. There should be enough water to fill the jars and still reach 1 to 2 inches above the tops of them. Bring the water to a boil and boil for 10 minutes. Leave the jars in the hot water until they are ready to be filled.

2. Prepare two-piece canning lids according to the manufacturer's recommendations.

3. Prepare sweet spread according to recipe and follow these general principles, adapted from the Clemson University Extension Service website·

To extract juice: Use only firm fruits naturally high in pectin. Select a mixture of about ¾ ripe and ¼ underripe fruit. Wash all fruits thoroughly. Crush soft fruits or berries; cut firmer fruits into small pieces. Using the peels and cores adds pectin to the juice during cooking. Put fruit and water (as instructed) in a large saucepan and bring to a boil. Then simmer according to times given or until fruit is soft. Stir to prevent scorching. One pound of fruit should yield at least 1 cup of clear juice.

When fruit is tender, strain through a colander into a bowl to remove seeds and skins, then strain juice again through four layers of cheesecloth or a jelly bag. Allow juice to drip through, using a stand or colander to hold the bag. Pressing or squeezing the bag or cloth will result in cloudy jelly.

To make jelly: Use 6 to 8 c. of extracted fruit juice at a time; double batches do not always jell properly. Measure juice and sugar. When a recipe is not available, try using ¾ c. sugar for each cup of juice. Test for pectin content using one of the following methods.

TEST FOR DONENESS

Cooking test: Measure ⅓ c. of juice and ¼ c. of sugar into a small saucepan. Heat slowly, stirring constantly until all the sugar is dissolved. Bring the mixture to a boil and boil rapidly until it passes the sheeting test: syrup forms two drops that flow together and "sheet," or hang, off the edge of the spoon. Pour the jelly into a clean hot jelly glass or a small bowl and let it cool. If the cooled mixture is jellylike, your fruit juice will jell.

Alcohol test: Add 1 tsp. of juice to 1 tbsp. of rubbing alcohol. To mix, gently stir or shake the mixture in a closed container so that all the juice comes in contact with the alcohol. DO NOT TASTE. The mixture is poisonous. Fruit high in pectin will form a solid jellylike mass that can be picked up with a fork.

Acid test: Test for acid using a simple taste test for tartness by mixing 1 tsp. lemon juice, 3 tbsp. water, and ½ tsp. sugar. If your fruit juice does not taste as tart as this mixture, it is not tart enough. Add 1 tbsp. lemon juice or ⅛ tsp. citric acid to each cup of fruit juice.

Temperature test: This is the most reliable of the doneness tests. First test the accuracy of the jelly or candy thermometer by placing it in boiling water to see if it measures 212 degrees F. Then place it in a vertical position into the boiling jelly mixture and read at eye level. The bulb of the thermometer must be completely covered with the jelly but must not touch the bottom of the saucepot. Boil mixture until it reaches

220 degrees F, which is 8 degrees F above the boiling point of water. (*Editor's note: This is for altitudes of 0 to 1,000 feet.*)

Sheet or spoon test: Dip a cool, metal spoon into the boiling jelly mixture. Raise the spoon about 12 inches above the pan, out of the steam. Turn the spoon so the liquid runs off the side. When the mixture first starts to boil, the drops will be light and syrupy. As the syrup continues to boil, the drops will become heavier and will drop off the spoon two at a time. The jelly is done when the syrup forms two drops that flow together and sheet, or hang off, the edge of the spoon.

Refrigerator/freezer test: Pour a small amount of boiling jelly on a plate and put it in the freezer for a few minutes. If the mixture jells, it should be done. During the test, the rest of the jelly mixture should be removed from the heat to prevent overcooking.

Editor's note: The procedures for making jellied spreads with commercial pectin vary somewhat from the above. With the addition of commercial pectin, it is not necessary to test for pectin, acid, or doneness. All-ripe fruit may be used for best flavor. Be sure to follow the manufacturer's directions carefully.

4. Remove the sterilized jars from the hot water one at a time, tilting to empty. To make sure they are completely drained, turn them upside down on a clean towel on the countertop. Turn right-side up and fill quickly with jelly mixture, leaving ¼ inch of head space. Wipe the sealing surface of the jars with a clean paper towel dampened with hot water to remove any of the mixture or sugar crystals. Work quickly to ensure that the filled jars stay as hot as possible until all are filled and ready to load into the canner for processing. Adjust lids.

5. Load the jars into the canner one at a time, using a jar lifter. Make sure to keep the jars upright at all times; tilting may cause the mixture to spill into the sealing area of the lid, which should remain clean and undisturbed. The water in the canner can be close to boiling when the jars are added, if the mixture has remained hot all the while.

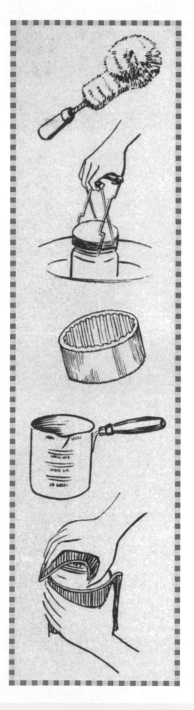

6. Turn the heat under the canner to its highest setting, cover the canner with its lid, and heat until the water boils vigorously. Then boil 5 minutes (altitudes of 0 to 1,000 feet). Butters and honey must be boiled for 15 minutes unless otherwise instructed (again, altitudes of 0 to 1,000 feet). The water level in the canner should be 1 to 2 inches above the tops of the jars and must remain boiling during the entire 5 (or 15) minutes of processing. Keep the flame high and the lid on.

7. When the jars have been processed in boiling water for the recommended time, turn off the heat and remove the canner lid. Wait 5 minutes. Remove jars from the canner using a jar lifter, again making sure to keep the jars upright. Place them on a towel or cooling rack, leaving at least 1 inch of space between them. Do not place jars on a cold surface or in a cold draft.

8. Cool jars upright for 12 to 24 hours to make sure they properly seal and that the mixture sets. Let the jars sit undisturbed during this time. Do *not* tighten ring bands on the lids or push down on the center of the flat metal lid until the jar is completely cooled, as this may cause seal failures.

9. Remove ring bands from the jars. Check to make sure the jars are properly sealed using one of the following methods recommended by the National Center for Home Food Preservation:

■ Press the middle of the lid with your finger. If the lid pops up when you release your finger, the lid is unsealed.

■ Tap the lid with the bottom of a teaspoon. If it makes a dull sound, the lid is not sealed. If the jar is sealed correctly, it will make a ringing, high-pitched sound.

■ Hold the jar at eye level and look across the lid. The lid should be concave in the center. If it is flat or convex, it may not be properly sealed.

You may opt to reprocess unsealed jars within 24 hours, using the original processing time. Or you may store them in the refrigerator, to use up within a few days, or the freezer, stored in freezer-safe plastic containers.

10. Wash jars and lids to remove all residues. Label, date, and store in a cool, dark, dry place out of direct sunlight. For best results, store between 50°F and 70°F; do not store at temperatures above 95°F or near heat sources like radiators. Likewise, do not store in any damp place or expose jars to freezing temperatures.

If a jellied spread is too soft after processing, you may remake it. Clemson University Extension lists these steps (*Note:* This is not applicable to sweet, unjellied spreads like butters and honeys, which are meant to be soft):

To remake cooked jelly or jam without added pectin: If the fruit juice was not acidic enough, add 1½ tsp. of lemon juice per cup of jelly

before boiling. Heat the jelly to boiling and boil until the jellying point is reached. Remove jelly from heat, skim, pour immediately into sterilized hot jars, and seal and process for 5 minutes.

To remake cooked jelly or jam with powdered pectin: For each cup of jelly or jam, measure 2 tbsp. sugar, 1 tbsp. water, and 1½ tsp. of powdered pectin. (Stir the package contents well before measuring.) Mix the pectin and water and bring to a boil, stirring constantly. Add jelly or jam and sugar. Stir thoroughly. Bring to a full rolling boil over high heat, stirring constantly. Boil hard ½ minute. Remove from heat, quickly skim foam off jelly and fill hot, sterile jars, leaving ¼-inch head space. Adjust new lids and process in a boiling water bath for 5 minutes.

To remake cooked jelly or jam with liquid pectin: For each cup of jelly or jam, measure 3 tbsp. sugar, 1½ tsp. lemon juice, and 1½ tsp. of liquid fruit pectin. Place jelly or jam in a saucepan and bring to a boil, stirring constantly. Quickly add the sugar, lemon juice, and pectin. Bring to a full rolling boil, stirring constantly. Boil hard for 1 minute. Remove from heat. Quickly skim off foam and fill hot, sterile jars, leaving ¼-inch head space. Wipe jar rims. Adjust new lids and process in a boiling water bath for 5 minutes.

It is always good practice to carefully examine all home-canned jars of food for signs of spoilage prior to opening and eating. If there is any mold on a jar of jam or jelly, or signs of other spoilage, discard the entire contents of the jar or container. Visit the National Center for Home Food Preservation website, **www.uga.edu/nchfp**, or call your local extension service agent if you have any questions at all about the safety of your home-canned products.

A final note about fruits for sweet spreads: Use only those that are high-quality, freshly picked, and blemish-free. This is a good rule to follow for both fruits and vegetables in all canned products.

PECTIN CONTENT IN FRUITS

To make successful jellies and jams, you must use at least some fruits in the mix that are high in pectin if you prefer not to use commercial pectin in order to achieve the proper jelling consistency. Some fruits also require the addition of acid, in the form of lemon juice, in order to jell.

Here is a chart of fruits high and low in pectin:

Group I

If not overripe, these fruits have enough natural pectin and acid for gel formation with only added sugar:

Apples (sour)	Currants	Loganberries
Blackberries (sour)	Gooseberries	Plums (all but Italian)
Crabapples	Grapes (Eastern Concord)	Quinces
Cranberries	Lemons	

Group II

These fruits are low in natural acid or pectin and may need the addition of either acid or pectin (or pectin-rich fruits):

Apples (ripe)	Elderberries	Loquats
Blackberries (ripe)	Grapefruit	Oranges
Cherries (sour)	Grapes (California)	
Chokecherries	Grape juice (bottle Eastern Concord)	

Group III

These fruits always need added acid, pectin (or pectin-rich fruits), or both in order to jell:

Apricots	Guavas	Rhubarb
Blueberries	Peaches	Raspberries
Figs	Pears	Strawberries
Grapes (Western Concord)	Plums (Italian)	

Jellies

GOOD LUCK IN JELLY MAKING

By Miriam J. Williams
June 1936

A friend said, "Why do recipes take so much for granted? When I first attempted to make jelly, do you suppose that I could find just how to start from any of the cookbooks around? [She didn't have a *Country Kitchen Cook Book*.] Without mother I was helpless.

"And," she added, "jelly-making is no fun when things don't go right, yet such a joy when luck comes your way."

The beginning cook may like to know, first of all, that jelly is defined as "a transparent, quivery mixture of fruit juice and sugar, which when unmolded holds its shape, tender, not syrupy nor tough."

My beginning jelly had none of those characteristics. I kept on boiling that mixture of plum juice and sugar with the hope that it would finally stiffen, only to make an unforgettably sticky mess. Lady Luck was certainly visiting some other home that day.

But need it depend upon luck? The definition above assumes that fruit juice contains all the properties necessary to make it "jell." And since not all fruits contain enough pectin and acid to make good jelly, we start first with learning something about the fruit itself. Some fruits have both acid and pectin, some just one or the other.

Fruits that belong in the pectin-rich group, provided they are not too ripe, are currants, grapes, crabapples, sour apples, quince, some plums and raspberries, blackberries, green gooseberries, and cranberries.

Fruits quite low in pectin are cherries, strawberries, rhubarb, sweet apples, peaches, pears, pineapple, and others.

If you wish to use fruit in the first class when it is quite ripe or those in the second group by themselves, there are both liquid and powdered forms of pectin available, accompanied by careful instructions of the whole jelly-making process. Not only is uncertainty avoided and boiling timing shortened by this method, but the range of fruit flavors which can be captured into delectable jellies has been greatly enlarged.

To make jelly without the addition of extra pectin requires, first of all, attention to the extraction of juice. Wash and slice large, hard fruits such as apples, quince, and plums. Remove any imperfect spots, but do not core or peel. Leave gooseberries and currants on the stem. Mash all berries and currants.

Add water as follows: apples, quince, and plums, equal amounts or weights of water and fruit, i.e., 1 quart water to 1 quart fruit. Gooseberries and currants, 1 weight or measure of water to 3 of fruit; 1 quart water to 3 quarts fruit. *(Editor's note: As of 2006, the NCHFP recommends the following: for apples, 1 cup water per pound of fruit; berries, none to ¼ cup water per pound of fruit; crabapples, 1 cup water per pound of fruit; grapes, none to ¼ cup water per pound of fruit; and plums, ½ cup water per pound of fruit).*

Cover and cook fruit at a rapid boil until just tender, 5 to 15 or 20 minutes, depending upon the fruit (quince takes much longer, up to an hour to soften). Strain through a jelly bag or several thicknesses of cheesecloth, first rinsed in cold water. Do not squeeze unless you make a second straining, or a cloudy gel will result. Some fruits are rich enough in pectin and acid to allow for a second extraction, but if this is done, juice should be concentrated somewhat before measuring for sugar. Grape juice should stand several hours or overnight to allow crystals to settle, then poured off or strained again.

Just how much sugar to add to extracted juice is important, for the tenderness and firmness of jelly depends upon the correct proportions of fruit acid, pectin, and sugar. In general ¾ cup of sugar for each cup of juice is a good rule, although fruits rich in pectin and acid, such as currants, gooseberries, crab apples, and some grapes, can take as much as a cup of sugar to each cup of juice. Too much sugar makes a soft, overly sweet jelly, while too little means a somewhat tough jelly.

Some fruits low in acid, such as quince, blueberries, and some apples, are better for the addition of a small amount of acid. *(See page 22 for information on acid testing.)*

Once juice is extracted and pectin and acid content tested, the fun of jelly making begins.

Do the actual boiling of juice and sugar in a large kettle so that a big surface of liquid is exposed for rapid evaporation. Unless you are following

special directions that come with pectin preparations, boil rapidly until the jelly test is reached (see page 22). One good test is to cook until two drops form simultaneously from the spoon and "sheet off" or break from the spoon. Another is to observe the "set" of a very small amount of juice on a cold saucer, but put the jelly kettle back from the heat until you are sure of the test. Skim just before pouring, then fill hot sterilized glasses or jars. Cover at once.

Some jellies do not reach their final stages of firmness until a week or more after they are made.

❧ Apple Jelly I
June 1936

Wash and slice tart fruit but do not core or peel. Add water to cover, which should be about an equal amount of fruit and water. Cook slowly to begin to extract juice, then bring to a rapid boil for 15 to 20 minutes or until fruit is soft. Strain. If a second extraction is made, squeeze bag to get out most of the juice and then put pulp back with an equal amount of water; boil rapidly for 10 minutes and let stand 10 minutes. Strain, squeezing out juice. Combine two extractions and strain without squeezing. Measure and concentrate, if necessary, so that there is about a pint of juice to each pound of fruit used. Test for pectin and acid. Add three-fourths as much sugar as juice, stir until dissolved. Boil rapidly until jelly test is reached, 3 to 5 minutes. Skim with a slotted spoon, pour, seal, and process.

❧ Apple Jelly II
January 1910

A very good and simple apple jelly guide is what I sometimes style my "hit or miss" recipe, not because it ever disappoints me, but because I have to fuss so little over it.

Select good, fair apples and put them on to boil, whole, and cook them until they burst. Then put them into a jelly bag (a large piece of cheesecloth serves the purpose) and let them hang several hours to drain. It does not do the least bit of harm to squeeze the bag a little, only not enough for the pulp to go through. Test for pectin and acid. Use nearly as much sugar as juice and heat the sugar in the oven before adding it. Boil the juice 20 minutes then add the heated sugar very slowly and boil rapidly until jelly test is reached, about 5 minutes. Skim, pack, seal, and process.

This jelly when cooled should be very clear and solid enough to cut with a knife. This recipe has never failed. This is a jelly that can be made in the winter, and it is well to keep it in mind, when the fruit closet begins to look empty and it is too early for fresh fruit.

—*H. M. Richardson*

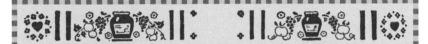

CRANBERRY SEASON ARRIVES

By Lucy Ann Fisher
November 1929

Cranberries are usually on the market four months of the year—from about the first of October through January. If you wish to keep them for later use, or prefer to buy fairly large amounts at a time during "open season," you will find it possible to prevent spoilage by [canning].

During the wintertime when most families are eating more meat than usual, cranberries with their freshness and tang make a particularly good garnish or main course accompaniment.

Cranberry jelly is good when chopped celery is added. (*Editor's note: A very small handful finely chopped, so as not to interfere with jelling, may safely be used.*)

❧ Cranberry Jelly
November 1929

1 qt. cranberries
2 c. water
2 c. sugar

Wash and pick over berries. Bring the water slowly to a boil then boil rapidly for 20 minutes. Rub the cranberries through a sieve or hang in a jelly bag; test for pectin and acid. Add sugar and boil rapidly until jelly test is secured, about 5 minutes. Skim, pack, seal, and process.

Variation: To make spiced Cranberry Jelly, tie 1 tbsp. whole cloves, 3 allspice berries, and 1 cinnamon stick into a spice bag. Boil with cranberries and remove before straining.

❧ Currant Jelly
June 1936

Wash and sort not-yet-ripe fruit, but do not remove from the stems. Measure and mash. To 3 qt. of fruit, add 1 qt. of water. Cook slowly to begin to extract juice, then bring to a rapid boil for 10 to 15 minutes. Rinse a jelly bag in cold water and use it to strain the currants. Measure juice—there should be about 1½ qt. If more than that amount, or a second extraction is made, concentrate down to 1½ qt. juice by boiling down rapidly. Test for pectin and acid, add 3 lb. (6¾ c.) of sugar—equal amounts of sugar and juice—and stir until dissolved. Boil rapidly in a large, broad kettle until the jelly test is reached. This should require not more than 5 minutes. Skim, pack, seal, and process.

❦ Currant-Raspberry Jelly
June 1938

Use fruit that is slightly underripe, or entirely ripe raspberries may be used with currants that are slightly underripe.

Wash currants (do not stem) and drain. Combine fruits, crush, and add ½ c. water to every 2 quarts of fruit. Bring slowly to a boil then boil rapidly 3 to 5 minutes, stirring frequently. Put in jelly bag and let drip through without pressing. Measure juice; test for pectin and acid. Put in a large kettle—do not boil more than 6 to 8 c. of juice at a time—and bring rapidly to a boil. Add sugar slowly, ¾ as much by measure as juice, stirring until all is dissolved. Cook very rapidly until the jelly test is secured. Remove at once; let stand a few seconds. Skim, pack, seal, and process.

❦ Elderberry Jelly
June 1927

3 qt. elderberries
3 qt. pared and sliced apples
4½ qt. sugar

Wash fruit well, barely cover with water, then bring slowly to a boil. Boil rapidly until soft. Strain through jelly bag, test for pectin and acid, measure juice, then add sugar (¾ c. per cup of juice) and cook juice rapidly until it responds to jelly test. Skim, pack, seal, and process.

❧ Grape Jelly
August 1912

Take part-ripe Eastern Concord grapes, wash well, add water in the amount of ¼ c. per cup of fruit. Bring slowly to a boil, crushing fruit, then boil rapidly until soft, strain, and let drip through a jelly bag. Test for pectin and acid. Rapidly boil juice 30 minutes, add a pound of sugar to a pint of juice, boil 8 minutes longer until done. Skim, pack, seal, and process.

Variation I: Substitute currants (¼ of which should be unripe), apples, or cranberries for the grapes.

Variation II: Venison jelly, a spiced jelly that is particularly good with wild game, makes a pleasant change from ordinary grape jelly. To the recipe above add 1 small piece of cinnamon and 24 whole cloves tied in a spice bag. Boil in juice and remove before packing.

❧ Green Grape Mint Jelly
July 1936

Wash but do not stem the green, unripe grapes of the red or purple variety, using no more than 6 to 8 c. per batch and weighing before cooking. Bring slowly to a boil with ¼ c. water per cup of fruit until they can be easily crushed, then crush them. To every 4 pounds of grapes add one bunch of fresh, crushed mint. Boil rapidly until grapes are soft, then strain juice through a jelly bag that's been rinsed in cold water. Test for pectin and acid. Measure juice. Add a pound of sugar to each pint of juice. Use a flat pan for rapid boiling and a brisk fire. Boil until jelly test is reached, about 12 minutes. Skim, pack, seal, and process.

HOW TO MAKE
YOUR OWN FRUIT PECTIN

August 1920

Editor's note: This is a labor-intensive process, when you add it to the time necessary to make jelly, but some contemporary jelly makers still swear by this process much favored by The Farmer's Wife.

When fruit juice will not jell, it is a good plan to combine it with other fruit—red currant with ripe raspberry, pineapple with apple are good combinations. Another plan is to make your own pectin.

Orange pectin: Cut or grate the orange rind from oranges; scrape out the remaining white rind and chop it. Mix ½ lb. white pith with 1 qt. cold water and 4 tbsp. lemon juice. Let stand 15 minutes then add 1 qt. water and boil 10 minutes. Let stand overnight in refrigerator, reheat, and boil 10 minutes. Strain and cool. Pectin may be used at once or stored in the refrigerator to use in jelly making within a couple of days. Add a sufficient quantity to any boiling juice to give a good pectin test, starting with ½ c. pectin to 2 c. juice and adding more if necessary.

Apple pectin: 1 lb. sour apples, skins and core, juice of 1 lemon. Cover with 1 qt. water and boil 30 to 45 minutes. Drain through a jelly bag without pressure. Use at once or refrigerate to use in jelly making the next day.

❧ Huckleberry Jelly
June 1927

6 qt. huckleberries
2 lemons
sugar

Clean fruit, slice lemons, and cook with crushed berries in small amount of water *(Editor's note: Use no more than ¼ c., depending on how juicy the fruits are)*, bringing slowly to a boil then boiling rapidly until soft. Strain through moistened jelly bag and test for pectin and acid. Measure juice, add sugar (¾ c. per 1 c. juice), and boil rapidly until mixture reaches the jelly test. Skim, pack, seal, and process.

■■■

❧ Peach Jelly
August 1912

Clean the peaches, which should be free stone peaches. Cut into quarters and weigh, using no more than 6 to 8 lbs. fruit per batch. Crack the stones and break the kernels. Put the peaches and 1 or 2 kernels into a kettle, add equal measure water to fruit. Bring slowly to a boil then boil rapidly until soft. Strain through a jelly bag and test for pectin and acid; you will probably need to add acid as well as homemade apple or orange pectin—see page 35. Allow 1 lb. sugar to a pint of juice. Boil rapidly about 20 minutes, skimming carefully. Pack, seal, and process.

■■■

❧ Plum Jelly
September 1920

2 c. plum juice, from about 1 lb. fruit
1¼ c. sugar

Cook plums by boiling them rapidly in ⅓ the amount of water as there is juice until tender. Strain through a clean muslin bag. Measure juice. Test for pectin and acid. Measure out ¾ as much sugar as juice and warm sugar in the oven. Boil juice 20 minutes then add warmed sugar. Boil another 3 to 5 minutes, until done. Skim, pack, seal, and process.

❦ Rhubarb (Pieplant) Jelly

June 1911

Old, tough stalks are best for jelly. Wash and cut up rhubarb without peeling. Bring slowly to a boil with a very little water (no more than ¼ c.) then boil rapidly until tender. Strain in a jelly bag, bring juice rapidly to a boil, and then add an equal amount of sugar as juice. Boil hard for 22 minutes and give the jelly test. Skim, pack, seal, and process.

PRACTICAL DEVICE FOR STRAINING JELLY

Mary E. Underwood
July 1911

Clean a plain wooden kitchen chair thoroughly, and then turn it, legs upward, on a kitchen table. Tie a clean, single or double piece of white cheesecloth securely by the corners to the chair legs, being careful not to allow too much fullness to prevent sagging. Place a bowl underneath the bag on the underside of the chair seat, and then pour some of the boiling water from the kettle into the bag. When it has run away and the cloth is still hot, quickly remove full bowl and put another in its place, and pour the hot fruit to be strained into the jelly bag. Then throw a clean, white mosquito netting over the chair and leave the jelly juice to strain. Of course, chair, table, floor, and every utensil used, as well as the cheesecloth and mosquito netting, must be scrupulously clean. I find this works to perfection, being much less troublesome than the old-fashioned jelly bag.

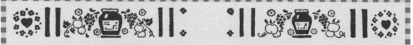

PRESERVING NATIVE FRUITS AND BERRIES

July 1935

In a woodsy northern county of Minnesota lives Mrs. E. P. Gibson, whose hobby is making the most of native fruits and berries. She has studied, classified, and experimented until her annual display of wild fruits at the St. Louis County Fair has brought special attention and recognition to their booth. Some of these fruits are captured in quivery jellies of deep hue and tangy flavor, some are . . . packed to preserve the original shape and texture, and others are turned into luscious jam and preserves.

Following are the experiences of native-fruit experimenters in several sections of the country. Of course, no suggestions are needed if you are fortunate enough to secure those extra-sweet wild strawberries or raspberries. Jam is the favorite way of preserving any that are not eaten "as is."

Editor's note: Contemporary canners may contact their local extension service for any available information about making jams and jellies from wild fruits readily available in their areas.

Preserving

❦ Chokecherry and Pin Cherry Jelly
July 1935

Wild cherries open the door to a new range of fruit flavors. Chokecherries are deservedly popular, for in spite of their low pectin content and astringent taste, they make choice juice, jams, and jellies when properly handled. The secret of jellying these and other puckery cherries is to combine with some mild, pectin-rich fruit such as apples, or to blend two or three extractions of juice when using with liquid or powdered pectin. Any tendency to bitterness is thus avoided and their truly fine flavor goes further.

Use ripe cherries, mash, and rapidly boil with ⅓ measure of water; make a second and even third extraction of the juice. Combine chokecherry juice with apple juice in equal proportions; test for pectin and acid. To each cup of mixed juice add ¾ c. sugar. Boil rapidly until jelly test is reached. Skim, pack, seal, and process.

❦ Juneberry Jelly
August 1924

6 qt. Juneberries
2 qt. rhubarb
sugar

Wash and pick over berries and dice rhubarb. Put fruit in kettle with just enough water to cover. Bring slowly to a boil then boil rapidly until fruit is soft and tender. Strain through a jelly bag and test for pectin and acid. Add an equal amount of sugar to the strained juice and boil rapidly until done. Skim, pack, seal, and process.

COMBINATIONS OF FRUIT JUICES THAT ARE PLEASING

Extract juice, combining in equal parts a rule.

Apple and strawberry, with a little lemon juice for flavor
Apple and cherry
Apple or currant and blackberry, with raspberry or elderberry
Apple and plum
Currant or apple and rhubarb
Apple and quince
Apple flavored with mint: Pour boiling water over mint leaves, equal
    parts. Let stand 1 hour. Use 2 tbsp. of mint extraction to each cup
    apple juice.
Apple flavored with rose geranium: Wash geranium leaves and put one
    in each jelly glass.

❦ Highbush Cranberry Jelly
July 1935

The American highbush cranberry matures with red or yellow fruit in late fall. The fruit is very rich in pectin, so it can be used alone or in combination with other fruits for jelly. Even fruit left hanging on the plants in winter makes a good quality jelly, according to a North Dakota bulletin on native fruits.

Select berries in the prime of ripeness, strip from stems, wash, and drain thoroughly. To each cup of berries use 1 c. of water. Boil from 3 to 5 minutes, mashing thoroughly with a wooden potato masher while boiling. Pour into jelly bag and allow to drip. To each cup of juice use ¾ c. of sugar, adding after the juice is hot. Boil rapidly until a soft jelly test is obtained (heavy drops and not a sheeting off). Pour hot jelly into hot sterilized jars. Seal and process. This jelly gets more firm in texture on standing.

JELLY STOCK FOR WINTER
Method of Simplifying Summer Work
Followed by Many Housewives

By Anna Coyle

In preparing for the winter's supply of jelly, what could be simpler than merely extracting the fruit juices during the busy fruit season and storing them in jars? The juice is called jelly stock. Each jar of stock is neatly labeled, giving such information as the kind of fruit, date prepared, and any facts that may assist in later making the best jelly. Jars of jelly stock are stored with other canned fruits and used as the demand arises.

❧ Apple Jelly Stock

Wash apples, cut in pieces, cores and all, and cover with water
After boiling point is reached, cook from 35 to 45 minutes.
Strain and pour juice into hot sterilized jars. Seal and process
5 minutes per pint/quart jar at altitudes of up to 1,000 feet.

❧ Apple Jelly Made from Stock

1 pt. apple jelly stock
1½ c. sugar

Heat to 222°F. Skim and pour into hot sterilized glasses. Seal
and process.

❧ Crab Apple Jelly

Cut apples in small pieces (no need to pare them), cover with water,
and when the boiling point is reached, cook for 35 minutes. Strain
through cheesecloth. Filter by pouring juice through a heavy flannel
bag and for each cup of juice use 1 c. of sugar. Crab apples contain
a good deal of pectin and are also very acidic. The jelly stage will be
reached between 220°F and 221°F. Skim, pack, seal, and process.
This jelly is very firm and excellent in flavor.

❧ Strawberry Jelly

Cap, wash, and crush berries; add only enough water to keep them
from burning. Cook at a rapid boil several minutes until soft and strain
juice through jelly bag. To 1 pt. strawberry juice add 1 pt. orange
pectin juice (see page 35) and bring to a boil; then immediately add
1 lb. sugar and cook to 223°F. Skim, pack, seal, and process.

EVEN STRAWBERRIES JELL PERFECTLY!

SURE-JELL *NEW*
POWDERED PECTIN PRODUCT
GIVES PERFECT RESULTS
WITH **ANY** FRUIT!

❧ Grape Jelly Stock

8 lbs. grapes (½ should be underripe)
1 qt. water

Crush grapes in water and boil for 20 minutes. Strain through cheesecloth and pour juice through a flannel bag. Pour into sterilized jars, seal, and process 5 minutes per pint/quart jar at altitudes of up to 1,000 feet. Store in a cool place until ready to make into jelly.

In grape jelly stock the crystals slowly settle to the bottom and by this method their crystallization in the jelly is reduced to a minimum. Orange pectin is frequently used with grape jelly stock to prevent the formation of crystals.

Variation: To make Muscadine Grape Jelly Made from Stock, proceed as in directions for grape jelly stock. Any of the following varieties may be used: Scuppernong, Thomas, Mish, James, Eden, Memory, Smith, Flowers, and Luola.

❧ Muscadine Grape Jelly Made from Stock

4 c. jelly stock
1 c. orange pectin (see page 35)
3¾ c. sugar

Combine jelly stock and orange pectin in a pan and bring to a boil. Add the sugar gradually and cook to 223°F. Skim, pack, seal, and process.

❧ Grape Jelly Made from Stock

Measure juice and add ¾ c. sugar for every cup juice. Heat to 223°F. Skim, pack, seal, and process.

❧ Blackberry Jelly Stock

6 qt. blackberries
1 pt. water

Wash berries and place with water over heat. After boiling point is reached, cook for 15 minutes. Strain through double cheesecloth, pack, seal, and process 5 minutes per pint/quart jar at altitudes of up to 1,000 feet. This will yield 3 pts. of jelly stock. Store in a cool place.

❧ Blackberry Jelly Made from Stock

2 pt. jelly stock
1½ lbs. sugar

Bring jelly stock to a boil and then add sugar gradually, stirring until completely dissolved. Cook to 222°F. Skim, pack, seal, and process.

❧ Ripe Gooseberry and Red Raspberry Jelly
June 1938

A rare instance where The Farmer's Wife *suggests the use of commercial pectin, to compensate for fully ripened fruit.*

1 qt. fully ripe gooseberries
½ c. water
1 qt. fully ripe raspberries
sugar
powdered fruit pectin, to follow manufacturer's recommendation

To prepare juice, crush thoroughly or grind gooseberries. Add water, cook slowly, then boil rapidly about 10 minutes. Crush thoroughly or grind red raspberries. Combine fruits; place in jelly cloth or bag and squeeze out juice. (If there is a slight shortage of juice, add small amount of water to pulp in jelly cloth and squeeze again.)

Measure juice into a large saucepan and place over hottest fire. Add sugar and pectin per the manufacturer's recommendation. Skim, pack, seal, and process.

Jams

Jams, unlike jellies, are made from the entire fruit, including seeds, and are not strained before boiling down and packing. Rather, cooked fruit with its juice is packed into jars and sealed. In the July 1928 issue, *The Farmer's Wife* states: "Jams are made from the whole berry fruits, including the seeds. These usually contain pectin, so that the fruit juice jellies; however, it is not cooked down as stiff as jelly. If part of the juice is removed for jelly making, the jam will be seedy and insipid. When dropped from a spoon, jam slowly sinks into a rounded mound."

Despite the differences between the two, jams require the same equipment as jellies (refer to beginning of this chapter), and they must also be packed hot into hot sterilized jars with ¼ inch of head space, and processed for 5 minutes in a boiling water bath. All suggestions about using fresh, clean, blemish-free fruit also apply, as well as boiling fruit rapidly to maintain pectin content. Some jam makers are less picky about jelling than others. If you prefer firm-jelling jams, use pectin-rich fruits or low-pectin fruits in combination with high. Or, use a commercial pectin according to the manufacturer's instructions.

❧ Apple and Plum Jam
June 1924

2 c. tart apples, diced
1 c. plums, stoned and cut
3 c. water
¾ c. sugar

Place the fruit in equal measure of water, crushing slightly to free part of the juice and prevent scorching. Slowly bring to a boil, then boil quickly until fruit is tender. Remove from heat to add sugar, then return quickly to a boil and cook until desired thickness, or until jelly test is achieved. Pack, seal, and process.

❦ Apple-Berry Jam
June 1924

Cooked and strained apple pulp from jelly making may be added to other fruits to thin out flavors of the more expensive varieties. The quality of the product is not lessened and often it is helped by such practice. Use ⅓ c. apple pulp to each quart of strawberries or raspberries, and 1 c. for blueberries, blackberries, or grapes. Boil all together with water equal in measure to berries and sugar in equal measure to all fruit til the jelly test is achieved. Pack, seal, and process.

❧ Berry and Small Fruit Jams
June 1938

To preserve the bright color and fresh flavor of the fruit, cook only 2 or 3 qt. at a time and boil rapidly over a hot fire, stirring constantly. At least ¾ of the fruit should be entirely ripe, but using a small proportion of underripe fruit will give a better consistency.

Good combinations are blueberries and black raspberries, red and black currants, currants and raspberries, gooseberries and blueberries or mulberries.

Wash and stem fruit and weigh or measure. Allow ¾ as much sugar as fruit *by weight* or ⅔ as much *by measure.* Place fruit in a kettle, crush to start the flow of juice. Bring slowly to a boil and boil rapidly for 5 minutes. Add sugar, stir until dissolved, and boil rapidly until as thick as desired, or until jelly test is achieved. Let stand a few minutes, stirring occasionally, and skim. Pack still hot, seal, and process.

Blackberry jam is preferred by some if the pulp is sieved, after the first cooking, to remove the seeds. Then measure and add sugar as directed.

❧ Blackberry Jam
August 1914

Only firm, solid fruit that is not overripe should be used for this purpose. Allow ¾ lb. of sugar to a pound of fruit, measured also and note number of cups of fruit used. Boil rapidly together with water in equal measure to fruit for 15 to 20 minutes, or until jelly test is achieved. Skim, pack, seal, and process.

Some prefer to use this fruit with ⅓ or ¼ of some other fruit. Pieplant (rhubarb) combined with black raspberries or blackberries makes a delicious jam. One housekeeper uses half berries and half pieplant or other fruit, another ⅓ berries to ⅔ pieplant with an equal amount of sugar.

❦ Strawberry Jam
June 1914

To every 2 pt. of very ripe strawberries add 1½ pt. of sugar. Mash together, stir well, and set over the fire to boil rapidly with an equal measure of water to fruit. Cook until thick, stirring to prevent scorching. Add lemon juice according to the directions on page 22. Pack, seal, and process.

Variation: For those who like more tart strawberry jam, some housewives would add currant juice, extracted from fresh currants instead of water to the above amount of fruit. Cook until jelly test is achieved. The addition of lemon juice will not be necessary.

■■■

❦ Strawberry and Pineapple Jam
June 1938

Slice ripe, washed berries and measure. Combine with an equal part of shredded pineapple (cooked, if fresh, to release some of its juice). Measure, add ¾ as much sugar and ⅓ measure of water to fruit. Boil quickly over a hot flame until thick and clear, stirring constantly, until jelly test is achieved. Pack, seal, and process.

■■■

❦ Gooseberry Jam
July 1935

Wild gooseberry jam is regarded as a choice spread. Spiced with cinnamon, nutmeg, and allspice, it makes an exceptionally fine meat accompaniment.

5 lbs. gooseberries, ½ green and ½ ripe
1¼ c. water
5 c. sugar

Wash gooseberries and remove stems. Mash and cook with water until skins are soft and juice is extracted. Measure out 5 c. juice, bring to a boil, then add sugar. Cook rapidly until it is of jellylike consistency (about 30 minutes). Pack, seal, and process.
—*Adapted from the University of Minnesota Extension Service website*

❦ Plum Jam with Ginger

August 1924

2 qt. pitted tart plums, chopped (*not* the Italian variety)
6 c. sugar
1-inch piece ginger root, peeled
¼ c. lemon juice
1½ c. water

Put all in kettle, bring slowly to boiling point; then boil rapidly with frequent stirring, until the consistency of marmalade. Skim, pack, seal, and process.
—*Adapted from the NCHFP website*

❦ Peach Jam

9 peaches
1 orange
sugar

Wash, peel, and stone peaches, and chop coarsely. Wash and chop orange, skin and all (remove seeds). Mix fruits and measure, adding an equal measure of sugar and no more than ¼ c. of water, if necessary, to prevent scorching. Bring slowly to a boil then boil rapidly until jelly test is achieved. Skim, pack, seal, and process.

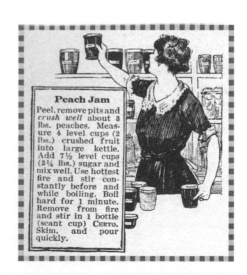

Peach Jam

Peel, remove pits and *crush well* about 3 lbs. peaches. Measure 4 level cups (2 lbs.) crushed fruit into large kettle. Add 7½ level cups (3¼ lbs.) sugar and mix well. Use hottest fire and stir constantly before and while boiling. Boil hard for 1 minute. Remove from fire and stir in 1 bottle (scant cup) Certo. Skim, and pour quickly.

THE BLUEBERRY SEASON

July 1920

July ushers in the blueberry season. This is one of the most desirable of the delicious wild fruits growing in the United States. Do not ignore the blueberries; get your share of the supply and store them, canned and preserved, alone and in combination.

Blueberries may be combined with rhubarb, raspberries, and strawberries. The acids of other fruits develop the flavor of this mild berry and though of excellent flavor when used alone, it is even better in combination.

❦ Spiced Blueberry Jam
June 1938

Editor's note: Here, with added commercial pectin.

4½ c. washed, stemmed blueberries
1 tsp. each cinnamon, cloves, and allspice
4½ c. water
7 c. sugar
liquid pectin, according to manufacturer's directions

Crush or grind fully ripe blueberries, add spices and sugar, and mix well. Bring to a rapid boil over a hot flame with an equal measure of water to fruit, stirring constantly. Add sugar and pectin according to manufacturer's instructions. Pack, seal, and process.

Conserves and Marmalades

Conserves are fruit products prepared by combining several different kinds of fruits which blend well. In a conserve, one fruit predominates in flavor, while there are also other fruits, raisins, orange peel, or nutmeats, which add desirable flavors and increase the food value of the product. Where small fruits are used in preparation, these are sometimes used whole, or they may be cut into small pieces, as is done with the larger varieties. Conserves are used as condiments and make excellent spreads for sandwiches or toast.

A marmalade is rightly an orange marmalade consisting of a clear tender jelly in which tender bits of orange peel are suspended, though generally it may include any fruit jam.

These fruit products should be brilliant in color, distinctive, and pleasing in flavor.

Equipment, packing, and processing for conserves and marmalades are identical to jellies and jams, unless otherwise noted. Follow instructions on pages 21–25. However, conserves can be cooked *slowly* all the while rather than rapidly boiled til fruit is tender, since jelling is not essential.

❧ Apple and Peach Conserve
June 1924

2 c. tarts apples, peeled and diced
2 c. peaches, peeled and cut in small pieces
½ c. orange juice and grated rind of ½ orange
¾ to 1 c. sugar
½ c. walnuts, if desired, cut in small pieces

Wash fruit, mix all ingredients but nuts in a saucepan, adding water if necessary to avoid scorching. Bring slowly to a boil then simmer til thick, 10 to 20 minutes adding walnuts for the last 5 minutes of cooking. Pack, seal, and process.

❦ Blueberry and Apple Conserve
July 1935

In place of the apple, another pectin-rich fruit used by some people is the small red haw or thorn apple. The juice extracted must be used in combination with juice from some more flavorful fruit.

1 qt. blueberries
1 qt. red haw or thorn apples, peeled and diced
6 c. sugar
juice of 2 lemons
grated rind of 1 lemon

Wash fruit well and combine ingredients; bring mixture to a boil then simmer until thick and clear, stirring and adding a small amount of water, if necessary, to prevent burning. Pack, seal, and process.

❦ Apple-Peach Conserve

3 c. peeled and diced tart apples
2 c. peaches that have already been
　　washed, stoned, chopped,
　　and cooked til tender
3 c. sugar
juice of 1 lemon

Mix all ingredients and simmer until thick and clear, stirring to prevent scorching. Pack, seal, and process.

❧ Cherry Conserve
August 1914

Stone and weigh the fruit and allow ½ lb. of sugar for every 1 lb. of fruit. Place together in a nonreactive bowl and let stand overnight in refrigerator. In the morning skim out the cherries and boil the juice for ½ hour. Add half the cherries; cook 15 minutes. Skim out and place in hot sterilized jars and keep hot. Cook remainder of cherries and skim out to hot jars; boil the syrup til thick and pour over cherries. This is Grandmother's old rule. Seal and store in refrigerator.

❧ Cranberry Conserve
November 1929

1 qt. cranberries
1 c. cold water
1 grapefruit, finely chopped
½ c. raisins, finely chopped
3 c. sugar
½ c. walnuts, chopped

Chop cranberries. Add cold water to grapefruit and cook until soft. Add cranberries, raisins, and sugar, and return to boil. Cook rapidly until thick. Add nuts during last 5 minutes of cooking and pack, seal, and process for 10 minutes per half-pint jar.

Variation: Substitute 2 oranges for grapefruit.
—*Adapted from the NCHFP website*

❧ Currant Conserve
August 1914

5 lbs. washed currants
½ c. seedless raisins, cut fine with scissors
juice, pulp, and chopped rind of 5 oranges
5 lbs. sugar

Boil slowly together 20 minutes until thick. Pack, seal, and process.

❧ Currant and Pineapple Conserve
July 1924

1 qt. red currants
2 c. grated pineapple juice and thinly sliced rind of 1 orange
4 c. sugar

Place currants and pineapple in no more than ¼ c. of water, crushing slightly to free part of the juice and prevent scorching. Add orange juice and rind, slowly bring to a boil, lower heat, and cook until tender. Remove from heat to add sugar, then return quickly to a boil and cook at low simmer until desired thickness. Pack, seal, and store in refrigerator.

❧ Gooseberry Conserve I
June 1924

5 lbs. gooseberries, ¼ unripe
4 lbs. sugar
½ c. raisins, chopped
juice and grated rind of 1 large orange

Wash fruit; mix ingredients. Bring to a boil and then simmer until fruit is soft and thick, adding a small amount of water if necessary to prevent scorching. Pack, seal, and process.

❦ Gooseberry Conserve II
June 1917

5 lbs. gooseberries, ¼ unripe
5 lbs. granulated sugar
2 lbs. raisins
juice of 4 oranges
½ c. water
½ c. walnuts, finely chopped

Remove stems and blossom ends of gooseberries and wash thoroughly. Place all ingredients except nuts in a kettle and cook slowly 1 hour; add a little more water if necessary to prevent scorching. Add nuts and cook until thick, stirring to prevent burning. Pack, seal, and process.

❦ Wild Gooseberry Conserve
July 1935

3 lbs. wild gooseberries
3 lbs. sugar
½ c. raisins
juice and grated rind of 3 large oranges

Wash the oranges and wash and stem the gooseberries. Combine juice and rind of the oranges with the gooseberries, then add sugar, raisins, and just enough water to keep the fruit from burning. Bring slowly to a boil then simmer until thick. Pack, seal, and process.

❦ Grape Conserve I
July 1924

5 lbs. Concord grapes, washed, skins removed and reserved
4 lbs. sugar
¼ tsp. salt
1 c. walnuts, finely chopped
1 c. raisins, chopped

Cook the grapes in water to cover until the seeds are loose. Put through a colander to remove seeds. Return to stove with sugar, raisins, and salt, and boil to thicken. Add grape skins and boil 10 minutes. Add nuts for the last 5 minutes of cooking. Pack, seal, and process.
—*Adapted from the NCHFP website*

❦ Grape Conserve II
June 1917

3 pt. Concord grapes
3 pt. sugar
1 pint water
juice of 2 oranges
½ c. raisins
½ c. walnuts, chopped

Wash grapes then press pulp from skins in a colander. Heat pulp through in a kettle, then press through colander to remove seeds. Cook pulp, skins, juice, raisins, and water together for 30 minutes. Add nuts and cook 5 more minutes. Pack, seal, and process.

❦ Peach Conserve
July 1924

A well-stocked preserve cupboard is a great comfort at all times and is especially appreciated when company comes.

4 lbs. ripe peaches
1 lb. grated pineapple
juice and rind of 1 orange
juice and rind of 1 lemon
3 lbs. sugar
½ lb. raisins, chopped
½ lb. blanched, slivered almonds

Wash the fruit, crushing slightly to free part of the juice and prevent scorching. Add orange and lemon juice with rinds. Slowly bring to a boil, lower heat, and cook until tender. Remove from heat to add sugar, then return quickly to a boil and cook until desired thickness, adding nuts and raisins for the last 5 minutes of cooking. Pack, seal, and store in refrigerator.

❧ Pinecot Conserve

November 1929

1 lb. dried apricots
2½ c. fresh pineapple, chopped
3 c. sugar
juice of 1 lemon

Soak apricots in water to cover overnight. Drain and chop, add pineapple and sugar, bring to a boil, and then cook for 15 minutes until thick. Add lemon juice. Skim, pack, seal, and store in refrigerator.

Note: Walnuts are good in this conserve, although not at all necessary.
—*Mrs. C. M. C., Pennsylvania*

❧ Plum Conserve

August 1918

4½ lbs. plums
6 c. sugar
chopped pulp from 2 oranges + ¾ c. thinly sliced orange peel
2 c. raisins
2 c. nuts, chopped

Wash, pit, and chop the plums. Mix with orange pulp, peel, sugar, and raisins, and cook together rapidly until as thick as jam, stirring to avoid scorching. Add the nuts 5 minutes before removing from the fire. Pack, seal, and process.
—*Adapted from the NCHFP website*

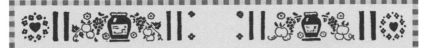

IN RHUBARB TIME
This Plentiful Spring Food Should Now Be Canned or Dried

By Lucile Wheeler
June 1918

Pieplant or rhubarb is one of the first fresh foods of spring. A part of the plentiful spring supply of rhubarb should be saved for autumn and winter. It may be canned in glass jars without sugar or made into conserves and confections. Rhubarb has the acid necessary for jelly making but lacks the pectin content, which is the second essential for a good jelly. *Make conserves instead!*

❦ Rhubarb Conserve I

6 c. rhubarb
1 orange
1 lemon
2 c. raisins
½ tsp. salt
1¼ c. water
5 c. sugar
½ c. walnuts, chopped

Wash and cut the rhubarb into ¼-inch pieces. Scrub the orange and lemon until rinds are perfectly free of soil and insects. Slice the orange and lemon into very thin sections, being careful to remove all seeds. Cook the rhubarb, orange, lemon, raisins, salt, and water until fruit is tender, stirring to prevent the fruit from burning if necessary. Add sugar and cook until thick like jelly. Add nuts and stir. Pack, seal, and process for 15 minutes for half-pint jars.

—*Adapted from the University of Alaska–Fairbanks Cooperative Extension Service website*

❧ Rhubarb Conserve II

4 lbs. rhubarb, cut in ½-inch pieces
1 lb. pineapple, chopped
5 lbs. sugar
¼ lb. walnuts, chopped
½ lb. raisins

Cook rhubarb and pineapple together slowly in no more than
¼ c. water for 30 minutes. Add remaining ingredients and cook
slowly til of jellylike consistency. Pack, seal, and store in refrigerator.

❧ Rhubarb and Orange Conserve
May 1928

9 c. rhubarb, washed and cut into 1-inch pieces
9 c. sugar
3 oranges

Divide rhubarb and sugar into 2 batches, mix in 2 nonreactive
vessels, and let stand overnight in refrigerator. In the morning
chop the washed oranges, rind and all, removing seeds. Turn all
the rhubarb and sugar into kettle, add orange, and stir gently until
blended. Cook 15 minutes, skimming as necessary, until thick.
Pack, seal, and store in refrigerator.

❧ Rhubarb and Nut Conserve

June 1914

3½ lbs. young, tender rhubarb
juice and grated rind of 2 lemons
¼ lb. hickory nuts or almonds, chopped

Wash but do not peel enough very young and tender rhubarb to make 3½ lbs. Add juice of 2 lemons and 3 lbs. of sugar and cook about 20 minutes, until thick. Then add ¼ lb. hickory nuts or almonds, chopped, and the grated rind of the 2 lemons, and cook 20 minutes longer, adjusting heat to prevent scorching. Pack, seal, and store in refrigerator.

❧ Rhubarb and Raisin Conserve

June 1917

2 qt. rhubarb, cut in ½-inch pieces
2 c. sugar
2 c. raisins, chopped
4 c. orange juice

Add sugar to rhubarb and let stand 4 to 5 hours then bring quickly to a boil. Add raisins and cook slowly for 1 hour, stirring frequently and adding a small amount of water if necessary to prevent scorching. Add orange juice just before removing from fire. Pack, seal, and store in refrigerator.

❦ Strawberry Conserve
August 1918

1 qt. strawberries, washed and hulled
½ lb. raisins
2 lbs. sugar
1 lemon
½ c. nuts, chopped

Grate the lemon peel and chop the pulp. Place all ingredients minus the nuts in a pan and cook over a slow, even fire until as thick as jam, adding a little water if necessary to avoid scorching. Add the nuts and cook 5 minutes longer. Pack, seal, and process.

❦ Strawberry and Pineapple Conserve
June 1917

3 pineapples, peeled, cored, and chopped
equal weight of strawberries, measured once pineapple is cut
sugar

Cook pineapple until tender in just enough water to prevent scorching. Wash, drain, and hull strawberries, cook until soft in a small amount of water and add to pineapple. Measure fruit and add ¾ the measure of sugar. Cook all together slowly until thick. Pack, seal, and store in refrigerator.

❧ Medley of Fruits Conserve
August 1918

2 lbs. peaches   1 lb. apples
1½ lbs. quinces   3 lemons
1½ lbs. pears   sugar

Wash, peel, and stone or core the fruit. Chop and weigh. For each pound of fruit allow ¾ pound of sugar. Put fruit and sugar in alternate layers in a nonreactive bowl and let stand overnight in refrigerator. Grate the rind from half the lemons and slice thin, then chop the pulp of all three lemons. Place the fruit and the lemon rind and pulp in a kettle and boil until mixture is as thick as jam, adding water if necessary to avoid scorching. Add 1 c. chopped nuts scalded briefly in boiling water then drained, if desired, 5 minutes before removing from the fire. Pack, seal, and store in refrigerator.

THIS IS MARMALADE MONTH

March 1924
To get a variety of flavors, a marmalade pattern is needed. Here is a good one:

    1 pt. sliced fruit
    3 pts. cold water
    1 lb. sugar for each pint of cooked fruit and water

Using the above as a basis, try in combination:

    1 lemon with 2 grapefruits
    1 lemon with 4 oranges
    1 lemon, 4 oranges, 1 pineapple

❧ Amber Marmalade
April 1922

The stock of cherry, plum, apple, and other preserves in the household is apt to be growing scarce. Citrus fruits, however, are available and the United States Department of Agriculture recommends the following easily made amber marmalade to increase the supply of sweets during the winter months:

1 orange, weighing 7 oz.
1 grapefruit, weighing about 1 lb. 3 oz.
1 lemon, weighing about 3 oz.
water
sugar

Select especially tender, clean, yellow, smooth-skinned fruit, free from blemishes. The thick-skinned varieties are better for this purpose than those having a thin, tough peel, since this thin peel is likely to become still tougher after cooking with sugar and acid. Wash the fruit well. Remove the skins and slice them very thin. Cook this peel in 1 qt. of cold water 3 times for 5 minutes each, discarding the water after each time.

Cut the fruit pulp into thin slices, removing the seed and the "rag" (pith). Combine this sliced pulp with the parboiled skins. To each weight or measure of fruit add 3 times its own weight or measure of water and boil for 25 minutes. Then add equal weight of measure of sugar and boil rapidly 25 minutes longer, or until the jelly stage is reached. Pack, seal, and process.

This marmalade should have a clear amber color, not at all of a brownish cast. It should be jellied throughout and the strips of peel which it contains should be transparent and tender. When larger quantities of fruit are used, longer periods of cooking will be necessary before the jelly stage is reached because of the larger amount of water which has to be evaporated by boiling.

❧ English Orange Marmalade
April 1913

6 Navel oranges
1 lemon
3 qt. water

Wash the oranges and lemon, slice very thin, removing and retaining seeds, then soak in 2 qt. of the water. Soak the seeds in the other quart of water. Next morning remove the seeds and mix the soaking water with the fruit in its water. Bring to a boil and boil 2 hours. Add 3 qt. sugar and boil 1 more hour, stirring gently. Pack, seal, and process.

This is the famous English Orange Marmalade.

❧ Lemon Marmalade
August 1914

Clean lemons with a brush, slice thin, and remove all seeds. To every pound of fruit add 3 pt. water. Let this mixture stand overnight in a nonreactive bowl in cool place. The next morning boil until tender and pour in a nonreactive bowl to stand 24 hours in refrigerator. Weigh and to every pound of fruit add 1½ lbs. sugar. Boil until syrup jellies and the lemon whites are translucent. Pack, seal, and process.

❧ Gooseberry and Orange Marmalade
August 1914

Combine together ⅔ gooseberries, ⅓ sliced oranges (washed with seeds removed), and sugar in equal amount to all the fruit. Cook gently until thick. Pack, seal, and process.

❧ Apricot Marmalade

1 lb. dried apricots
1 qt. water
2 oranges, washed and chopped fine
1 lemon, washed and chopped fine
about 6 c. sugar

Soak apricots in the water for several hours. Drain apricots and chop fine. Mix together the apricots, oranges, and lemon, adding all citrus juices and peel. Add sugar, stir, and cook rapidly til thick. Pack, seal, and process.

SEE OUR SHELVES FILLING WITH SUMMER'S PRICELESS FRUITS

By Lucy D. Cordiner
August 1920

Is it not a delight, some early autumn evening, to take Father and the Boys down to the cellar to show them the shelves well stocked with jellies, jams, and marmalades, with canned fruits and canned vegetables in every kind and combination, and to hear Father say in his most appreciative manner, "Well, Mother, you've already done more than your share to supply us with food for the winter," and then to hear one of the boys say, "I've read that we must eat vegetables and fruits if we are to keep very well and strong; *we* should be the 'wellest' family in the township next winter, Mother," and then the baby—"Gee, marmalade!"

❦ Concord Grape Marmalade

Wash grapes, drain and remove stems. Pop the grapes from skins. Cook pulp slowly til seeds separate, then rub through a strainer. Add skins to pulp, measure, and add ¾ measure of sugar to fruit. Mix and cook slowly for 30 minutes, til thick. Pack, seal, and process.

❦ Rhubarb Marmalade

May 1913

6 c. rhubarb, cut in small pieces
6 c. sugar
2 large or 4 small oranges cut in thin slices, skin and all
   (remove seeds)

Boil all together until thick. Pack, seal, and store in refrigerator. This will be found delicious.

❧ Rhubarb and Fig Marmalade
June 1911

6 lbs. rhubarb, peeled and cut
1 lb. fresh figs, chopped
¼ lb. lemon peel, cut fine
1 tbsp. bottled lemon juice
5 lbs. sugar

Combine rhubarb, fresh figs, lemon peel, and bottled lemon juice. Cover all with 5 lbs. of sugar and let stand in a nonreactive bowl until the next day in refrigerator. Then boil slowly for 1 hour. Pack hot in hot sterilized jars, seal, and store immediately in the refrigerator, to use within a week.

❧ Rhubarb and Date Marmalade
August 1914

Cook chopped and peeled rhubarb in water to cover until tender, drain, and add an equal amount of pitted dates. Weigh and add an equal quantity of sugar and no more than ¼ c. of water so it will not stick and will dissolve the sugar. Cook slowly until thick. Pack, seal, and store in refrigerator.

Variations: Equal quantities of strawberries, cherries, and gooseberries with the same amount of sugar will make a delicious marmalade.

❦ Rhubarb and Orange Marmalade
August 1914

Use 3 lbs. rhubarb and 3 large Navel oranges. Grate rind of
1 orange, slice and remove division skins from all 3. Cover
oranges and rhubarb with 3 c. sugar and let stand overnight in
a nonreactive bowl in the refrigerator. In the morning bring to a
boil then cook slowly until thick. Before finishing add 3 more cups
sugar. Pack, seal, and store in refrigerator.

❦ Pineapple Plus Marmalade
August 1926

Do not try to make too large an amount of marmalade at a
time as it is likely to change in flavor if cooked the longer time
necessary for a large quantity.

1 qt. finely cut rhubarb
3 qt. diced pineapple
3 qt. sugar
3 oranges

Let pineapple and rhubarb stand with the sugar overnight in
refrigerator. Remove rind from oranges, slice it fine, cook in water
to cover until tender, then add with sliced orange pulp to rest of
the fruit. Cook about 30 minutes, until desired consistency. Pack,
seal, and store in refrigerator.

❧ Plum Marmalade
August 1914

Scald and skin ripe plums and remove pits by halving. Allow 1 lb. sugar to every pint of pulp. Mix and let stand 15 minutes then boil rapidly for 20 minutes. Skim, pack, seal, and process.

❧ Quince Marmalade
August 1914

Peel and core the fruit, cut in fine pieces and stew in equal measure of water until tender, at least 1 hour, then add ¾ lb. sugar to every pint of fruit. Boil 20 minutes til thick. Pack, seal, and store in refrigerator.

❧ Peach Marmalade I
August 1914 and August 1928

Peach marmalade is delicious; use choice, luscious, ripe peaches.

Remove peach skins by dipping in boiling water. Cut in halves or quarters, remove pits, and measure fruit. Cook 6 qt. peaches and 1 qt. water for 1 hour, then add 3 qt. sugar and cook 45 minutes. Pack, seal, and process.

❧ Peach Marmalade II
August 1920 and April 1938

Remove peach skins from 10 lbs. peaches by dipping in boiling water.
Cut in halves or quarters, remove pits, and chop with 3 orange rinds
very coarse. Add an equal measure of sugar and cook for 2 hours.
Pack, seal, and process.

❧ Harlequin Marmalade
June 1935

1 qt. strawberries, hulled and sliced
1 qt. cherries, pitted
1 qt. currants
1 qt. red raspberries
1 qt. gooseberries
5 lbs. sugar

Bring to a slow boil, crushing as you go; once juice forms and sugar
dissolves, boil rapidly til clear and thick, about 10 to 20 minutes. Pack,
seal, and process.

❧ Florida Carrot Marmalade

March 1924

3 c. carrots
½ tsp. salt
2 oranges
3 lemons
4 c. sugar
1 c. water

Wash carrots, scrape, grind, or chop fine, then cook in salted water to cover until tender; drain. Wash and peel oranges, chopping the rind of one and cutting the rind of the other into fine strips. Boil rinds til tender, in water to cover; drain. Cut the orange pulp in small pieces. Squeeze the juice from the lemons. To the hot carrots add sugar, allowing it to melt. Then add 1 c. water, lemon juice, orange pulp, and cooked peel. Cook until syrup is thick and fruit is clear. Pack hot in hot, sterilized jars and store immediately in refrigerator, using up within a week.

Variation: Some people like to add spices in the proportion of 1 tsp. each of cinnamon, ginger, and allspice.

❧ Quick Orange Marmalade
March 1924
This recipe calls for commercial pectin.

2 oranges
1 lemon
7 c. water, divided
sugar
liquid pectin

Wash fruit and remove skins in quarters. Place the skins in a pan, cover with 4 c. water, and boil 20 minutes. Drain and with a sharp-edged spoon scrape out desiccated white part of skins. With sharp knife cut yellow rind as thin as possible in pieces 1 inch long. Simmer in 2½ c. water in covered saucepan 15 minutes. Drain. Slice fruit, discard seeds, add ½ c. water, and simmer in covered saucepan 45 minutes. Add rinds and measure. There should be 2 c. Add water if necessary to get this amount. Follow manufacturer's directions for adding sugar and pectin.

❧ Apple and Tomato Marmalade
August 1926

No up-to-date processing information exists for this delicious recipe, so amounts have been halved from the original, allowing you to make a batch that can be used up quickly when storing in the refrigerator. Apple pulp left over after juice has drained off for jelly may be used.

1½ c. apple pulp
1½ c. strained tomatoes—peeled and pressed through colander
1¼ c. sugar
1 stick cinnamon
½ tbsp. whole cloves
⅛ c. vinegar

Press apple pulp through coarse strainer, add tomatoes and sugar. Tie spices in cheesecloth and boil 30 minutes with fruit. Add vinegar; boil 10 minutes more. Remove spices. Pack hot in hot, sterilized jars; seal and store immediately in refrigerator, using up within a week.

Butters and Honeys

An article in the July 1928 issue of *The Farmer's Wife* explained the basics of preparing fruit butters and honeys for canning:

> Fruit butters are delicious and should be in every home as accompaniments for puddings and so forth.
>
> Fruit butters are made from the fleshy part of the larger fruits, as pears, plums, and apples, from which the skin and seeds have been discarded. Lacking pectin, it does not jell, but is cooked down until thick enough to spread on bread.
>
> There should be no large particles of fruit or lumps. The fruit butter is not too thick and sticky. The flavor is of fresh fruit, not too sweet, too spicy, scorched, or disagreeable from cooking in a tin pan. The color must be bright and sparkling, not too dark, not colorless.
>
> Remove all skins and seeds by putting the pulp through a colander. Use ½ as much sugar as fruit and boil slowly until very thick and smooth, stirring constantly. Pack, seal, and process.
>
> Nonjellied spreads like butters and honeys should be packed hot in half-pint or pint jars; leave ¼ inch of head space when packing. Unless otherwise instructed, process butters and honeys for 15 minutes in a boiling water bath. (*Editor's note: This time is for altitudes of 0 to 1,000 feet; contact one of the resources listed at the end of this book, or your local extension service agent, for processing times that are correct for your altitude.*)

❧ Apple Butter
July 1924

8 lbs. apples, chopped but not peeled
    or cored
2 c. sweet cider
2 c. vinegar (5 percent acidity)
2 tsp. ground cloves
2 tsp. ground allspice
3 tsp. ground cinnamon
2½ c. white sugar
2½ c. brown sugar

Cook apples slowly in cider and vinegar until tender. Press through colander, then cook pulp slowly with spices and sugars until very thick. Pack, seal, and process for 5 minutes.
—*Adapted from the NCHFP website*

❀ Apple Tomato Butter

6 c. apple pulp left over from jelly making
6 c. cooked, strained tomatoes
5 c. sugar
4 sticks cinnamon
2 tbsp. whole cloves
½ c. vinegar

Press apple pulp through a coarse strainer. Add tomatoes and sugar, then tie spices in a spice bag. Boil together for 30 minutes, add vinegar, boil another 10 minutes, then remove spice bag. Pack, seal, and store in refrigerator.

❀ Apple-Quince-Cranberry Butter
June 1924

2 c. apple pulp
1 c. quince pulp
1 c. cranberry pulp
2½ c. sugar

Mix apples, quince, and cranberries, heating slowly to the boiling point while crushing slightly. Cook slowly 1½ to 3 hours, until very thick. Pack, seal, and store in refrigerator.

❧ Wild Plum Butter

July 1935

Pit plums and cook in hot water (1 c. per each quart fruit) until soft. Remove skin by pressing pulp through a coarse sieve or strainer. Measure pulp and add ⅔ measure of sugar. Mix and cook slowly to butter consistency. Sprinklings of cinnamon, allspice, and ground cloves may be added if desired. Pack, seal, and process for 15 minutes.

❧ Plum Butter

September 1920

3 lbs. plums
1 lb. sugar
1 tbsp. cinnamon

Use any multiple of this proportion.

Wash plums, cover with boiling water and a pinch of baking soda, and let stand 5 minutes. This treatment removes much of the bitter taste sometimes associated with plums. Drain and again cover with boiling water and cook until tender. Cool, remove seeds, and to every 2 lbs. of pulp add 1 tbsp. cinnamon and 1 lb. sugar. Cook until thick, about 1 hour. Pack, seal, and store in refrigerator.

This makes a delicious butter.

❦ Pear Honey
November 1929

Pare and core 8 lbs. of pears. Cook in water to cover til soft, then strain through a jelly bag or cheesecloth. Measure juice and return to stove; bring to a rapid boil. Add ½ measure of sugar as juice, then boil again til of a honey-like consistency. Pack, seal, and process for 15 minutes.

❦ Pear Pineapple Honey
1934

8 lbs. pears
1 pineapple, peeled, cored, and finely chopped
sugar

Wash, pare, and core pears. Chop; add pineapple. Cook in water to cover til soft, then strain through a jelly bag or cheesecloth. Measure juice and return to stove; bring to a rapid boil. Add ½ measure of sugar as juice, and then boil again til of a honey-like consistency. Pack, seal, and process for 15 minutes.

Other Preserved Fruits and Fruit Products

The farmer's wife canned fruit in abundance, from her own fields and orchards. And she canned them immediately after picking, to ensure peak flavor and freshness. A fine solution for contemporary canners with no gardens of their own is to purchase fruit in-season from local farmers at area farmers' markets, and to can it within twenty-four hours. Make sure you select fresh, firm fruits at the peak of ripeness, in excellent condition. Do not use moldy or spotty fruit. Also make sure that fruit is carefully washed free of all dirt. *Note:* In this chapter, all methods, procedures, and recipes (except refrigerator recipes) have been checked for safety against the following sources: NCHFP website, University of Georgia Extension Service website and Clemson University Extension Service website.

The Basics

There are all sorts of ways to can fruit: cooked or raw, hot or cold, or in water, juice, or syrup. *The Farmer's Wife*, most assuredly, favored syrup, as evidenced by the recipes in this chapter. But you can try your hand at other, less sweet, methods. Below is a chart of syrups from the NCHFP's website as well as methods for packing fruit, in syrup or not, from the University of Georgia Extension Service home canning.

The equipment you will need for preserving fruits and fruit products is similar to that for sweet spreads (page 19). Please consult that list. However, you will not need such specialized equipment as a thermometer or a jelly bag. Pint and quart jars, rather than half-pint jars, are the preferred size here. Likewise, please consult the sweet spreads chapter for notes on how to clean and sterilize jars, pack the canner, remove jars from it, and cool and store jars (pages 21–25).

Note: The processing times outlined in this chapter are for hot water bath canners, used at altitudes of 0 to 1,000 feet. If you live at an altitude of above 1,000 feet, please consult the National Center for Home Food Preservation website (**http://www.uga.edu**) or your own local extension service for recommended processing times.

Since fruit products are processed for longer times than sweet spreads, it will be necessary to occasionally check the boiling water canner to make sure that the jars inside are completely covered. Add more BOILING water as necessary to ensure this.

Before eating any food that you have canned, it is important to check jars for signs of spoilage. A bulging lid or leaking jar is a sign of spoilage. So is spurting liquid, a bad odor, or mold. Dispose of all spoiled canned fruit in a place where it will not be eaten by children or pets.

Adding syrup to canned fruit helps to retain its flavor, color, and shape. Although it does not prevent its spoilage, which is why it is important to follow packing methods and processing times exactly. A "very light" syrup approximates the natural sugar content of many fruits. The quantities of water and sugar listed below make enough syrup for a whole canner load of pint or quart jars. This means nine pint jars or seven quart jars.

To make the syrups for hot packs of fruit (the preferred method of *The Farmer's Wife*), bring water and sugar to boil, add fruit, reheat to boil, and pack immediately into clean jars that have been kept hot in hot water. Empty the canner according to instructions on pages 24–25 (jams and jellies).

Very light syrup: ½ c. sugar per quart of liquid = 4½ c. syrup

Light: 1 c. sugar per quart liquid = 4¾ c. syrup, for already very sweet fruit

Medium: 1¾ c. sugar per quart liquid = 5 c. syrup, for sweet apples, berries, cherries, grapes

Heavy: 2¾ c. sugar per quart liquid = 5⅓ c. syrup, for tart apples, apricots, sour cherries, gooseberries, nectarines, peaches, pears, plums

Very heavy: 4 c. sugar per quart liquid = 6 c. syrup, for very sour fruit

The following list of processes with process times is taken from the University of Georgia Cooperative Extension website (**http://www.fcs.uga.edu/ext/pubs/fdns/FDNS-E-43-01.pdf**) unless otherwise indicated. All these fruits were favored by *The Farmer's Wife* and appeared on its pages over the years; this list, however, updates procedures for safety.

■■

❧ Apple Juice, Hot Pack

For best results, buy fresh juice from a local cider maker within 24 hours after it has been pressed, or press your own. Refrigerate juice for 24 to 48 hours. Without mixing, carefully pour off clear liquid and discard sediment. Strain clear liquid through a paper coffee filter or double layer of damp cheesecloth. Sterilize jars and keep hot. Heat juice, stirring occasionally, until juice begins to boil. Pour into hot jars, leaving ¼ inch of head space.

Pints and quarts: 5 minutes

❦ Apples, Hot Pack

Make a very light, light, or medium syrup. Wash, peel, core, and slice apples. Place in a large saucepan. Add 1 pint syrup, water, or juice per 5 lbs. apples. Boil 5 minutes, stirring occasionally. Pack hot apples into hot jars, leaving ½ inch of head space. Fill jar to ½ inch from top with hot syrup.

Pints and quarts: 20 minutes

❦ Applesauce, Hot Pack

Wash, peel, and core apples. Place in an 8- to 10-quart pot. Add ½ c. water. Stirring occasionally to prevent burning, heat quickly, and cook until tender (5 to 20 minutes, depending on maturity and variety). Press through a sieve or food mill, if desired. If you prefer chunk-style sauce, omit the pressing step. If desired, add ⅛ c. sugar per quart of sauce. Reheat sauce to boiling. Pack into hot jars, leaving ½ inch of head space.

Pints: 15 minutes; quarts: 20 minutes

❦ Apricots

Apricots can be packed in very light, light, or medium syrup. They can also be packed in water, apple juice, or white grape juice. Prepare the liquid and keep it hot. Dip fruit in boiling water for 30 to 60 seconds until skins loosen. Dip quickly in cold water and slip off skins. Cut in half, remove pits, and slice if desired.

Hot Pack

In a large saucepan heat fruit in syrup, water, or juice to a boil. Pack hot fruit into hot jars leaving ½ inch of head space. When packing halves, place them cut-side down. Fill jars to ½ inch from the top with hot liquid.

Pints: 20 minutes; quarts: 25 minutes

Raw Pack

Pack raw, sliced fruit into hot jars, leaving ½ inch of head space. When packing halves, place them cut-side down. Fill jars with hot liquid, to ½ inch from the top.

    Pints: 25 minutes; quarts: 30 minutes

❧ Berries

Not cranberries or strawberries
Berries may be canned in water, juice, or syrup. Prepare and heat the liquid of your choice. Wash, drain, cap, and stem berries. For gooseberries, snip off heads and tails with scissors. See specific instructions for canning cranberries, below. Strawberries are thought these days to keep much better frozen, so there are no standard recommendations for canning them.

Hot Pack

Blueberries, currants, elderberries, gooseberries, and huckleberries
Heat to boiling about 1 gallon of water for each pound of berries. Blanch berries in boiling water for 30 seconds. Drain. Place ½ c. of hot syrup, juice, or water in each hot jar. Pack hot berries into hot jars, leaving ½ inch head space. Fill jars to ½ inch from top, with more hot syrup, juice, or water.

    Pints and quarts: 15 minutes

Raw (use for any of the berries)

Place ½ c. of hot syrup, juice, or water in each hot jar. Fill jars to ½ inch from the top with raw berries, shaking gently while filling. Add more hot syrup, juice, or water, leaving ½ inch head space.

    Pints: 15 minutes; quarts: 20 minutes

❦ Cherries

Stem and wash cherries. Remove pits if desired. If pitted, treat with a little lemon juice to prevent darkening. If cherries are canned unpitted, prick skins on opposite sides with a clean needle to prevent splitting. Cherries may be canned in water, apple juice, white grape juice, or syrup. Heat to boiling the liquid of your choice.

Hot Pack

In a large saucepan add ½ c. water, juice, or syrup to each quart of drained fruit. Bring to a boil. Pack cherries in hot jars, leaving ½ inch head space. Fill jar to ½ inch from top with hot liquid.

Pints: 15 minutes; quarts: 20 minutes

Raw Pack

Add ½ c. hot water, juice, or syrup to each hot jar. Fill jars to ½ inch from the top with drained cherries, shaking down gently as you fill. Add more hot liquid, leaving ½ inch of head space.

Pints and quarts: 25 minutes

❦ Cranberries, Hot Packs

Make a heavy syrup. Wash and remove stems from cranberries. Carefully but quickly add cranberries to boiling syrup. Boil 3 minutes. Fill fruit into hot, clean jars, leaving ½ inch of head space. Cover with boiling syrup, leaving ½ inch of head space. Remove air bubbles and adjust head space if needed. Wipe rims of jars with a dampened clean paper towel; adjust two-piece metal canning lids.

Pints and quarts: 15 minutes

—*Adapted from the NCHFP website*

❦ Fruit Purée, Hot Pack

Any fruit but figs, bananas, asian pears, melons, papaya, mango, or coconut

Stem, wash, drain, peel, and remove pits from all fruits, as necessary. Measure fruit into large saucepan, crushing slightly if desired. Add 1 c. hot water for each quart of fruit. Cook slowly until fruit is soft, stirring frequently. Press through sieve or food mill. If desired, add sugar to taste. Reheat pulp to boiling. If sugar was added, boil until it dissolves. Pack purée into hot jars, leaving ¼ inch head space.

   Pints and quarts: 15 minutes

Peaches: Follow directions and processing times for apricots, on pages 84 and 85.

❦ Pears, Hot Pack

Prepare a very light, light, or medium syrup, or heat apple juice, white grape juice, or water. Wash and peel pears. Cut lengthwise in halves and remove core with a melon baller or metal measuring spoon. Boil pears 5 minutes in syrup, juice, or water. Pack hot into hot jars, leaving ½ inch of head space. Fill jars to ½ inch from top with hot liquid.

   Pints: 20 minutes; quarts: 25 minutes

❦ Plums

Prepare a very light, light, or medium syrup. Stem and wash plums. To can whole, prick skin on two sides of plums with fork to prevent splitting. Freestone varieties may be halved and pitted.

Hot Pack

Add plums to hot syrup and boil 2 minutes. Cover saucepan and let stand 20 to 30 minutes. Pack hot plums into hot jars, leaving ½ inch of head space. Fill jars with hot syrup to ½ inch from the top.

Pints: 20 minutes; quarts: 25 minutes

Raw Pack

Pack raw plums firmly into hot jars, leaving ½ inch of head space. Fill jars with hot syrup to ½ inch from the top.

Pints: 20 minutes; quarts: 25 minutes

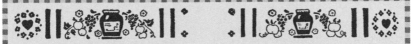

DELICIOUS RECIPES FOR SMALL FRUIT

By Elma Iona Locke
June 1910

❦ Preserved Black Raspberries

The large, juicy varieties of black raspberries are especially rich and delicious when canned. For each quart jar, boil 1 c. water and ½ c. sugar together for a few minutes to make a medium-heavy syrup. Scald 2 qt. nice ripe washed berries in boiling water for 30 seconds; a long cooking will make them hard. Stand hot sterilized jar in the boiling water while you fill it with the boiling fruit, then add syrup, leaving ½ inch of head space. Seal can with lid as soon as it is filled. Process 15 minutes.

❦ Preserved Currants, Without Cooking

Green currants are canned by the cold process by simply placing in hot sterilized pint jars, pouring over ½ c. boiling water or syrup to cover, leaving ½ inch of head space. Seal and process pints for 15 minutes.

❦ Preserved Cooked Currants

Mix 2 c. sugar with 4 c. water for each pound of currants, to make a medium-heavy syrup. Blanch currants in boiling water for 30 seconds, then drain. Pack into clean hot jars then add ½ c. boiling syrup, leaving ½ inch of head space. Seal and process pints or quarts for 15 minutes.
—*Adapted from the NCHFP website*

❦ Currant Bar-le-Duc

June 1914

The original, nearly defunct recipe for *Bar-le-Duc,* originating with fourteenth-century French monks, is only approximated here. To be authentic, this would require the addition of rare white currants and the removal, by hand with a hollow goose quill, of each currant's seeds. Not a recipe for the faint of heart! There is no contemporary tested recipe for this admixture of ingredients, so plan to store in the refrigerator without processing and to use up in a timely fashion.

3 qt. ripe red currants
2 qt. sugar
1 c. honey

Let currants and sugar stand overnight in refrigerator. In the morning add honey and boil 25 minutes. Pack hot in hot, sterilized jars, and seal and store immediately in refrigerator, using up within a week.

❦ Blackberry Nectar
July 1935

Wash 12 lbs. of well-ripened berries and crush thoroughly. Add 1 qt. of boiling water and let stand 12 hours or overnight in a cool place. Next morning strain through a muslin bag. Let drip thoroughly but do not squeeze. To each measure of this liquid add an equal amount of sugar and ¼ c. bottled lemon juice. Bring to a boil. Pack hot into hot, sterilized bottle, leaving ¼ inch of head space. Process 10 minutes. When ready to serve, add 3 tbsp. of this liquid to a glass of crushed ice and water. Sweeten to taste.

—*Adapted from the University of Minnesota Extension Service website*

❧ Favorite Strawberry Preserves
June 1936

From Arkansas, a strawberry state, comes the favorite recipe of Gertrude Conant, extension nutritionist at Little Rock, a recipe that Arkansas women like.

Wash and then hull the berries. Weigh out 2 lbs. of the berries into a rather shallow pan that is still large enough so that the juice will not boil over. Cover the berries with 1¾ pounds of sugar, shake it over the heat until the juice has issued freely, then place over a high flame and boil *briskly* for 10 minutes. Let stand overnight in the juice in refrigerator, so the berries will plump up, then reboil quickly, and pack hot in hot, sterilized jars. Store immediately in refrigerator and use up within a week.

These preserves have the original flavor of the fresh berries due to their not being cooked a long time, and no water is used in connection.

❧ Preserved Strawberries
June 1912

Strawberries require a little more sugar than other fruits in canning in order to keep well. I have heard a good many complaints from housekeepers in regard to their fruit not keeping well but where ½ lb. sugar to 1 pound of berries has been used, the results were always good.

The dark colored berries are best. They should be fresh and not too ripe, also cleaned and stemmed. Combine 6 c. strawberries

with 4½ c. sugar and let stand overnight in refrigerator. Bring to a boil, stirring gently, and boil 15–20 minutes til thick. Pack hot in hot, sterilized half-pint jars, pouring syrup over fruit to cover and leaving ¼ inch of head space. Seal and process 5 minutes.
—Mrs. E. B. Wightman
—Adapted from the NCHFP website

❦ Strawberry Syrup
July 1911

Use 6½ c. of the fruit that is ripest for syrup. Wash and remove caps and stems and crush in a saucepan. Bring to boil then simmer 10 minutes, til soft. Strain, then strain juice again through jelly bag or double layer of cheesecloth. To 5 c. juice add 5 c. sugar; boil then simmer 1 minute. Skim and pour into hot, sterilized jars, leaving ½ inch of head space. Process half-pints or pints 10 minutes in boiling water bath.

Variation: The same method may be used for blueberries, cherries, grapes, and raspberries.
—Adapted from the University of Minnesota Extension Service website

❦ Strawberry Cordial
June 1914

To each gallon of cleaned and hulled strawberries add 1 qt. of water; boil 10 minutes and strain. Add 2 tsp. whole allspice and 2 sticks cinnamon tied in a spice bag. Boil 20 minutes more, remove spices, and funnel hot into hot, sterilized jars or freezer-proof containers; seal and store immediately in refrigerator or freezer.

❦ Strawberry Wine
June 1914

1 gallon strawberries
1 qt. water
1½ pt. sugar
juice of 2 oranges

Crush the berries, add the water, sugar, and juice. Boil 15 minutes, strain, pour hot into hot, sterile jars or freezer-proof containers; store immediately in refrigerator or freezer.

❦ Cherry Preserves
June 1935

2 pt. pitted cherries
3 pt. sugar
2 qt. water

Rinse cherries and put in kettle, cover with sugar and add 2 qt. water. Heat very slowly at first to bring to a boil. Then boil rapidly 12 minutes. Pack fruit in hot, clean pint jars, pouring over hot syrup to cover and leaving ½ inch of head space. Process for 15 minutes.
—*Adapted from the NCHFP website*

USING OUR WILD FRUITS

By Mrs. Floyd Luros
August 1924

"What a delicious sauce! What is it?" asked a friend of mine one day when I served at tea some of my favorite wild plum sauce. This same friend had always turned up her nose at her wild fruit. My husband always insisted that my wild plum sauce was better than all the rest, and the pies I made with my canned Juneberries rivaled any he had eaten in the best hotels, so I had always put up an abundance of these.

We farmers in the Northwest, losing for the last three years on our wheat crops, can no longer afford to depend wholly on shipped-in fruits. So, by necessity, some of us have turned to the neglected wild fruits in our woods, and we have found that we can make just as delicious sauces, jams, and jellies as before. First comes the wild gooseberry, which should be picked when underripe.

❧ Berry Juices

The best fresh fruit flavors are obtained if the juice is extracted from freshly picked fruit. Pick over fruit, crush, add a very little water—about 1 to 2½ c. to 3 qt. of fruit. Heat until fruit is tender and soft, about 15 minutes, stirring often. Strain through a jelly bag. Pour off juice carefully to avoid disturbing any sediment. Bring to a boil again. Pour into hot, clean pint bottles, leaving ¼ inch of head space. Seal and process for 10 minutes.

❦ Preserved Cranberries
November 1912

To each quart of cranberries use ¾ pt. of water and 1 lb. sugar to make a heavy syrup. Heat the sugar in the water and when it boils, add the cranberries. Cook slowly until skins crack, about 5 minutes. Pack hot berries in hot, clean pint or quart jars, then add syrup to cover, leaving ½ inch of head space. Seal and process for 15 minutes.
—*Adapted from the NCHFP website*

❦ Wild Juneberry Sauce

To those who have not tasted Juneberries, I will say that they are supposed to be a cross between the blueberry or huckleberry and the chokecherry. They grow on bushes ranging from 3 to 8 feet in height, and the berries are larger and darker than blueberries and have a richer flavor. This flavor is brought out more markedly in canning when one part of rhubarb is used with two parts Juneberries. The rhubarb also makes the berries tender. In the winter this sauce makes delicious pies, like a two-crust blueberry pie.

6 qt. Juneberries
2 qt. rhubarb
3 lbs. sugar
3 qt. water

Carefully wash and pick over berries and dice rhubarb. Put sugar and water in kettle, bring to boiling point, skim, then boil gently without stirring for 10 minutes. Add fruit, bring to boiling point, and simmer gently until rhubarb is cooked up and berries are tender. Pack fruit hot in hot, clean pint jars, topping off with boiling syrup to cover, leaving ½ inch of head space. Seal and store in refrigerator.

❧ Apple "Catsup"
September 1918

1 qt. homemade apple sauce,
    according to directions on
    page 76 (apple butter)
1 tsp. ginger
1 tsp. cinnamon
1 tsp. cloves

1 pt. 5 percent vinegar
1 tsp. pepper
1 tsp. mustard powder
1 tsp. onion extract
2 tsp. canning or pickling salt

Simmer slowly til thick, 10 to 20 minutes. Pack in hot, clean pint jars, leaving ¼ inch of head space, and seal with new, clean lids. Process for 15 minutes.

❧ Mixed Currant "Catsup"
June 1914

3 lbs. red currants
2 lbs. black currants
3 lbs. sugar
1 tbsp. cloves
1 tbsp. each cinnamon, allspice, black pepper, salt
1 c. vinegar at 5 percent acidity (see page 22)

Stem the currants, wash, weigh. Then cook them as for jelly, rubbing the pulp and juice through a fine sieve. Add sugar, vinegar, and spices. The spices may be whole or ground as desired. If left whole, tie in thin muslin bags. Boil til thick as desired. If using whole spices, remove muslin bag. Pack hot in hot, clean half-pint or pint jars, leaving ¼ inch of head space. Seal and store in refrigerator.

❦ Spiced Gooseberry Preserves

July 1933

1 qt. ripe gooseberries
1 qt. sugar
1 tbsp. vinegar
⅛ tsp. cloves
1 tsp. cinnamon
½ tsp. allspice

Mix together. Bring slowly to a boil and boil 20 minutes. Pack hot in hot, clean half-pint or pint jars, leaving ¼ inch of head space. Seal and store in refrigerator.

❦ Wild Gooseberry Catsup

August 1924

5 lbs. wild gooseberries
4 lbs. sugar
2 c. cider vinegar
1½ tbsp. cinnamon
1 tbsp. cloves
1 tbsp. allspice

Wash and stem berries. Place in kettle and add sugar, vinegar, and spices. Bring to boiling point; simmer gently for about 2 hours. Pour hot into hot, clean half-pint or pint jars, leaving ¼ inch of head space. Seal and store in refrigerator.

❦ Elderberry or Wild Grape Catsup

July 1935

Rich and spicy.

2 qt. ripe elderberries or grapes (stemmed)
vinegar at 5 percent acidity, to cover
1 c. sugar
1 tbsp. each cinnamon, cloves, allspice
¼ tsp. cayenne

Cook fruit until barely soft in vinegar. Rub through sieve; add sugar and spices. Cook until thick like ordinary tomato catsup. Pour hot into clean, hot half-pint jars, seal and store in refrigerator.

❦ Spiced Grape Catsup

September 1925

This is excellent with most meats but especially so with game and wild fowl. The grapes are better for this purpose if half are green.

7 lbs. grapes
1 c. vinegar
2 tsp. cinnamon
3 lbs. sugar
1 tsp. cloves
1 tsp. allspice

Wash, stem, and pop grapes from skins. Put into cooking dish over fire with a small amount of water. When pulp is soft enough

to let seeds come free, rub through colander. Bring to a boil and continue cooking until tender. Add remaining ingredients and cook until mixture thickens, 20 to 30 minutes. It will require almost constant stirring toward the last as it should be quite stiff when cold. Pack hot into hot, clean half-pint or pint jars. Seal and store in refrigerator.

❦ Wild Grape Juice
July 1935

Wild grapes are treated much the same way as the cultivated fruit. These fruits are best in flavor when picked quite ripe.

Pick grapes when ripe (the riper the grapes, the better the flavor). Wash the bunches carefully, removing dried up and green grapes and cutting away excess stems. Put bunches in a large pan to a depth of 2 inches or so. Add boiling water to cover. Heat but keep from boiling. When seeds begin to come out, strain juice through cheesecloth. Press lightly but do not squeeze. Allow to sit in refrigerator 24 hours in order to let sediment settle. Reboil, taking care to leave sediment behind. Pour hot into hot, clean pint or quart jars, leaving ¼ inch head space. Seal and process 5 minutes.

To serve, dilute to taste with water, sweeten slightly, and serve ice cold. The juice of ½ lemon may be added to a pitcherful.
—*Adapted from the NCHFP website*

❦ Peach Preserves

August 1912

Dip fine ripe peaches in boiling water to remove skins, halve them, and remove the pits. Make a syrup of 4 c. water to 1 c. sugar per pound of prepared peaches. Boil sugar and water together. Remove scum and add fruit, cook 10 minutes, remove peaches to clean, hot pint jars, leaving ½ inch of head space. When all the fruit is in the jars, pour over hot syrup, leaving ½ inch of head space. Seal and process 20 minutes.

The peculiar peach flavor is better preserved if a few kernels are used. Crack the pits, removing the kernels; remove the skin by pouring boiling water over them. Put 1 or 2 into each jar.

Editor's note: There is no evidence to support this claim, but you may add 1 or 2 peach kernels if desired. DO NOT eat kernels, and DO NOT use more than 1 or 2 per jar as they are toxic at high doses.
—Adapted from the NCHFP website

❦ Preserved Pears

September 1913

6 c. sugar
8 c. water
2-inch knob fresh ginger, peeled
8 lbs. pears, peeled, quartered, and cored
8 lemons

Dissolve the sugar in water and ginger over high flame, boiling til thickened, then add pears, juice of 8 lemons, and grated peel of 1 lemon. Cook until pears are tender, remove to hot, clean pint jars, discarding ginger and pour syrup over pears, leaving ½ inch of head space. Seal and process for 20 minutes.
—Adapted from the NCHFP website

❧ Pear Preserves
1934

16 c. diced pears
13 c. sugar
2 tbsp. almond extract

Pare and halve pears and scoop out cores. Make syrup of a ratio of
½ c. sugar to 4 c. water per pound of pears. Boil syrup, then add
pears and extract, and boil all together for 5 minutes. Remove from
stove and pack hot into clean, hot pint jars, leaving ½ inch of head
space. Seal and process for 20 minutes.
—*Adapted from the NCHFP website*

❧ Wild Plum Catsup
August 1924

5 qt. wild plums
5 tsp. baking soda
4 lbs. sugar
1 pt. vinegar
1 qt. water
1½ tbsp. cinnamon
1 tbsp. ground allspice
1 tbsp. ground cloves

After thoroughly washing and picking over the plums, put them
in a kettle with boiling water to cover them and add baking soda.
Cooking with soda removes the bitter taste. As soon as the plums
begin to break open, remove from the liquor, cool slightly, and
squeeze out the stones. Boil sugar, vinegar, water, and spices then
add pitted plums. Bring to boiling point and simmer gently for
about 30 minutes. Strain. Pack hot in hot, clean half-pint or pint
jars, leaving ¼ inch of head space. Seal and store in refrigerator.

❦ Kansas Preserves
August 1910

The flavor of this preserve might be too strong and bitter for some palates; additionally, there is no recommended processing time for the mixture. Therefore, make this preserve in a small batch and store in the refrigerator, using up within a week.

1 pt. light sorghum syrup
1 tbsp. fresh butter
1 tsp. minced fresh ginger root or ground ginger
1 tsp. ground cinnamon
1 tsp. lemon peel, chopped fine
1 tsp. orange peel, chopped fine
2 peach leaves (optional)
wild plums, pieplant (rhubarb), crabapples, or any native fruit
2 c. sugar, heated in oven

Boil light sorghum syrup very rapidly for 15 minutes, being careful not to let it scorch by lifting the pan from the fire when it boils up. Add, for each pint of syrup, 1 tbsp. of fresh butter. Tie in a thin, muslin cloth a teaspoon each of grated ginger root or ground ginger, cinnamon, lemon peel, orange peel, and two peach leaves. Boil up then add wild plums, pieplant (rhubarb), crabapples, or any native fruit, and 2 c. of sugar heated in the oven. Boil rapidly until the fruit is tender, about 20 minutes. Pack hot in hot, sterilized jars, seal, and store immediately in refrigerator, using within a week to 10 days.

❦ Canned Pineapple
July 1911

Wash and quarter the pineapple, peel, and cut out the eyes. Then cut into small dice. Weigh the fruit and juice. To every pound of pineapple allow ½ c. of granulated sugar. Stir and boil sugar and water (in a ratio of 4 c. water per ½ c. sugar) together, then add fruit and simmer 10 minutes. Pack hot in clean, hot pint jars, cover with syrup, leaving ½ inch of head space. Seal and process for 15 minutes.
—*Adapted from the NCHFP website*

❦ Dried Apricots with Pineapple Preserve
April 1922

The Department of Agriculture has tested and approves the following recipe for a good winter preserve. The children will like it for their school lunches and to many persons it will prove a novelty for Sunday night supper.

Soak 1 lb. chopped dried apricots in water to cover overnight in refrigerator. Drain. To 1 lb. chopped fresh pineapple add ½ lb. sugar and cook steadily for 20 minutes. Add the apricots with another ½ lb. sugar and cook rapidly 10 minutes longer. This preserve requires careful watching to prevent scorching. Pack hot in hot, sterilized jars, seal, and store immediately in refrigerator, using up within a week.

❦ Plum Sauce
September 1920

September is the month for plums.

This recipe has been handed down to the third generation by a grandmother who was a famous cook. This is another refrigerator preserve.

1 qt. plums
pinch baking soda
1 c. sugar
1 tbsp. flour

Wash plums, place in stew kettle, cover with boiling water, add baking soda, and let stand on the back of the stove for 5 minutes. Drain and cover again with boiling water and boil until tender. Add sugar and flour, stir to combine, and let boil up thick. Pack hot into hot, sterilized jars. Seal and store immediately in refrigerator and use within one week.

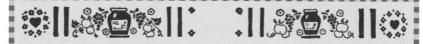

WE ARE CANNING PRUNES

By Miriam J. Williams
May 1935

"Canning prunes? I never heard of *that* before!" It wasn't the words so much as the tone of voice that made me hasten to explain to visitors who stepped into *The Farmer's Wife* Country Kitchen the day we were experimenting with canned prunes.

Purchased in 25-pound boxes, prunes are a very good buy this spring. Here is another good reason for prune-canning—the best flavor of dried prunes is secured with long standing in juice *after* they are cooked. Haven't you found that the prunes at the bottom of the big blue bowl, well covered with juice, are the best of the lot?

On the diner of a famous railroad, the chef serves only choice prunes, plump, tender, and juicy. His secret is that he cans them, soaking them first 12 to 18 hours in water to cover. He then packs the fruit in clean, hot jars, heating the juice in which they were soaked after adding a very little sugar and a bit of stick cinnamon.

Editor's note: There are no up-to-date recommendations for processing canned prunes. Therefore, store this delicious concoction in the refrigerator and use up within a week. The Farmer's Wife *favored them for winter breakfasts.*

Soak the prunes. Then make:

🥄 Pickling Syrup for Prunes

2 c. prune juice, from the soaking
2 c. vinegar
2 c. brown sugar
4 3-inch pieces stick cinnamon
2 tsp. whole cloves
1 tsp. allspice berries

Tie spices in a bag and heat with liquid and sugar to boiling. Add soaked prunes and simmer 30 minutes. Pack prunes and syrup into clean, hot jars, seal, and store in refrigerator.

❦ Wild Yellow or Red Plum Sauce
August 1924

There seem to be two varieties: the larger yellow sugar plum and the smaller red ones. The yellow sugar plum is the best for making sauce.

4 lbs. plums
1 tsp. baking soda
3 c. sugar
1 small piece ginger, minced
1 tbsp. salt
1 c. vinegar

After thoroughly washing and picking over the plums, put them in a kettle with boiling water to cover them and add baking soda. Cooking with soda removes the bitter taste. As soon as the plums begin to break open remove from the liquor, cool slightly, and squeeze out the stones. Place plums, sugar, ginger, salt, and vinegar in kettle, bring to boiling point, then simmer slowly until tender, about 1½ hours. Care should be taken not to cook them too long as then they will not be as attractive or delicious. Pack hot in hot, clean pint jars, leaving ¼ inch of head space. Seal and store in refrigerator.

❦ Pumpkin Preserve
March 1924

❄

Editor's note: Pumpkin, a low-acid and dense food, is tricky to can. At present, the USDA has no safely tested recipes for processing pumpkin preserves; therefore, these should be stored in the refrigerator or freezer.

2 c. sugar pumpkin, peeled and cut
   in squares
1 c. sugar
½ c. cold water
1 lemon sliced thin, seeds removed

Mix and let stand in nonreactive
bowl overnight in refrigerator then cook til clear. Pack hot in
hot, sterile jars and store immediately in refrigerator or freezer.
Consume within one week.

Pie Fillings

The farmer's wife canned fruit a-plenty for wintertime pie making. Often, she canned fruit straight or in syrup and adjusted to make it into a filling worthy of pie once she opened the jar. The following recommendations and recipes for pie fillings (except for rhubarb) are adapted from the National Center for Home Food Preservation website, adapted from the excellent bulletin "Complete Guide to Home Canning." These fillings use a cornstarch product called Clear Jel™ to achieve their thick consistency, a product available through some canning supply stores. Each recipe is for 7 quarts—1 quart per 8- or 9-inch pie. Processing times are for a boiling water bath.

AND NOW COMES RHUBARB!

By Gertrude Shockey

The drift at the gate's melted low,
The garden's nearly free from snow;
Amid leafy mulch, pink hearts sun-kist;
And here's rhubarb again on the list!

Just in time to gratify that craving for something fresh—nature's own call for a blood cleansing and a blood purifying after a winter's heating dishes—comes rhubarb!

Certainly it requires an abundance of sugar to make it pleasingly palatable, but if we use the earliest grown stalks, we will find them not nearly so sour or strong, as the later grown.

Canned Rhubarb for Sauce and Pies
June 1918

Wash rhubarb and cut in ½-inch pieces. Cook with sugar in a ratio of ½ c. sugar per 4 c. fruit, bringing to a boil. Pack at once into hot, clean pint or quart jars, leaving ½ inch of head space. Seal and process for 15 minutes.

❧ Apple Pie Filling

6 qt. firm, crisp, tart apples, such as Stayman, Golden Delicious,
　　or Rome
5½ c. sugar
1½ c. Clear Jel
1 tbsp. cinnamon
2½ c. cold water
5 c. apple juice
¾ tbsp. bottled lemon juice (or more, up to 1 c., to taste)

Wash, peel, and core apples then slice in ½-inch slices; blanch 6 c.
apples at a time in 1 gallon boiling water for 1 minute. Drain, keeping
hot fruit in covered bowl while remainder is blanched. Combine
sugar, Clear Jel, cinnamon, water, and apple juice in a large kettle.
Cook on medium-high heat until mixture thickens and bubbles. Add
lemon juice and boil 1 minute, stirring constantly. Mix in apples then
pack immediately in hot, clean pint or quart jars, leaving 1 inch of
head space. Seal and process for 25 minutes.

❧ Green Tomato Pie Filling

4 qt. green tomatoes, chopped
3 qt. tart apples, peeled and chopped
2 lbs. seedless raisins
¼ c. lemon or orange peel, minced or grated
2 c. water
2½ c. brown sugar
2½ c. white sugar
½ c. vinegar at 5 percent acidity (see note on page 22)
1 c. bottled lemon juice

2 tbsp. cinnamon
1 tsp. nutmeg
1 tsp. ground cloves

Combine all ingredients in a large kettle and cook over low heat, stirring often, til tender and thick (35 to 40 minutes). Pack in hot, clean quart jars, leaving ½ inch of head space. Seal and process for 15 minutes.

❦ Cherry Pie Filling

6 qt. fresh cherries, washed, stemmed, and pitted
7 c. sugar
1¾ c. Clear Jel
9⅓ c. cold water
½ c. bottled lemon juice
2 tsp. almond extract, if desired
1 tsp. cinnamon, if desired

Blanch cherries, 6 c. at a time, in 1 gallon of boiling water for 1 minute. Drain, keeping blanched fruit in covered bowl. Combine Clear Jel, water, and flavorings in a large kettle and cook over medium-high heat until thick and bubbly. Add lemon juice and boil 1 minute, stirring constantly. Mix in cherries then pack immediately in hot, clean pint or quart jars, leaving 1 inch of head space. Seal and process for 30 minutes.

Preserved Tomatoes and Tomato Products

The tomato was one of the most important crops in a farmer's wife's garden. She canned it whole or in pieces to use in later, winterbound recipes; she canned it in the form of soups and sauces; she canned it as catsups and spicy condiments to serve along with roasts.

The Basics

Tomatoes canned alone can be processed either in a hot water bath or a pressure canner. Pressure canner times are shorter and yield a more nutritious product, but a full load must be packed into the canner at one time, which makes small-batch canning impossible. A full canner load is comprised of 7 quarts or 9 pints. An average of 21 pounds of whole or halved tomatoes (and 22 pounds of crushed tomatoes) is needed for 7 quarts. An average of 13 pounds (and 14 pounds of crushed tomatoes) is needed for 9 pints. A bushel weighs 53 pounds and yields 15 to 21 quarts, an average of 3 pounds per quart.

If you only want to can a few pints or quarts of tomatoes, a boiling water bath is the clear choice. However, all tomato products that are packed with another vegetable MUST be processed in a pressure canner to ensure safety. A bit further on in this chapter you will find recommendations and recipes from the NCHFP website to start off that great late-summer tradition of canning "Friend Tomato." They are similar to tomato products from *The Farmer's Wife's* own kitchen, with updates for safety.

Only vine-ripened tomatoes in perfect condition should be used for canning. Further, the USDA recommends that you DO NOT use tomatoes from dead or frost-killed vines. To ensure the proper acidity of canned whole, crushed, and juiced tomatoes, add BOTTLED lemon juice: 2 tbsp. per quart and 1 tbsp. per pint, which can be added to the jars just before packing. You can substitute double that amount of vinegar with a 5 percent acidity, although you may not like the flavor. You can add ½ tsp. per pint and 1 tsp. per quart of salt for flavor.

Remember that the processing times listed in this book are for altitudes of 0 to 1,000 feet. If you live at a higher altitude, contact your local extension service agent for the processing times that are correct for your altitude.

Following are some notes on pressure canners, adapted from the Clemson University Extension Service website:

The *Clostridium botulinum* microorganism is the main reason pressure canning is necessary for processing some tomato products, as well as all vegetables and products that contain meat, poultry, and fish. Though the bacterial cells are killed at boiling temperatures, they can form spores that can withstand these temperatures. These spores grow well in low-acid canned foods in the absence of air. When the spores begin to grow, they produce deadly *botulinum* toxins. These spores can be destroyed by canning food at a temperature of 240 degrees Fahrenheit or above for the correct length of time. This temperature is above the boiling point of water so it can only be reached in a pressure canner.

A pressure canner is a specially made heavy pot with a lid that can be closed to prevent steam from escaping. The lid is fitted with a vent (or petcock), a dial- or weighted-pressure gauge, and a safety fuse. Newer models have an extra cover lock as an added precaution. It may or may not have a gasket. The pressure canner also has a rack. Because each type of canner is different, be sure to read the directions for operating your canner and keep them for future reference. Two types of pressure canners are recommended for home use: the weighted-gauge pressure canner and the dial-gauge pressure canner. Make sure you know what type you have and that it is clean and in good working order. If you are uncertain how to test, maintain, or use your pressure canner, be sure to contact your local extension service agent for assistance.

Here is how Clemson University recommends canning and processing tomatoes and tomato products:

Gather tomatoes early, when they are at their peak of quality. Do not use overripe, decayed, or damaged tomatoes, or tomatoes picked from frost-killed vines. Gather or purchase only as many as you can handle within two or three hours. Wash the tomatoes carefully, handling small amounts at a time. Lift them out of the water, drain the water, and continue rinsing until the water is clear and free of dirt. Dirt contains some of the bacteria that are most difficult to kill. Don't let the tomatoes soak, though; they will lose flavor and nutrients. The cleaner the raw tomatoes, the more effective the canning process.

Examine jars and discard those with nicks, cracks, and rough edges. These defects will not permit an airtight seal on the jar, and food spoilage will result. All canning jars should be washed in soapy water, rinsed well, and then kept hot. This could be done in the dishwasher or by placing the jars in the water that is heating in your canner. The jars need to be kept hot to prevent breakage when they're filled with a hot product and placed in the canner for processing. Jars that will be filled with food and processed for fewer than 10 minutes in a boiling water bath canner need to be sterilized by boiling them for 10 minutes. *Note:* If you are at an altitude of 1,000 feet or more, boil an additional minute for each 1,000 feet of additional altitude. Jars processed in a boiling water bath canner for 10 minutes or more or in a pressure canner will be sterilized during processing. Be sure to use new two-piece lids. Follow the manufacturer's instructions for treating them. Some need to be brought almost to a boil and then left in hot water, while others need to be boiled for a period of time. (See directions on pages 23–24 (the sweet spreads chapter) for more detailed instructions.)

Tomatoes may be packed raw, or they may be preheated before packing. The hot pack yields better color and flavor, especially when the tomatoes are processed in a boiling water bath. For both raw pack and hot pack, there should be enough syrup, water, or juice to fill in around the tomatoes in the jar and to cover them. If not covered by liquid, the tomatoes at the top tend to darken and develop unnatural flavors. It takes from ½ to 1½ c. of liquid to adequately fill a quart jar.

A bubble freer is a useful tool for tomato and vegetable packing, allowing you to remove air from jars before sealing.

Raw pack: For this method put raw, unheated food directly in jars. Pour boiling water, juice, or syrup over the food to obtain the head space specified in recipe. Tomatoes packed raw should be packed tightly because they will shrink during processing.

Hot pack: For this method, heat the tomatoes to boiling (or for specified time) and then pack along with boiling hot liquid in hot jars. Tomatoes packed hot should be packed fairly loosely, as shrinkage has already taken place.

Steps for Boiling Water Bath Method

Fill the canner about halfway with hot water. Turn on the burner and heat the water.

For raw-packed jars, have the water in the canner hot but not boiling to prevent breakage of the jars when they're placed in the canner. For hot-packed jars, use hot or gently boiling water.

Fill the jars as described in raw pack or hot pack methods on page 116.

Allow the proper head space, as indicated in each recipe. This is necessary so that all the extra air will be removed during processing, and a tight vacuum seal will be formed.

To make sure that air bubbles have not been trapped inside the jar, run a bubble freer or any plastic or rubber utensil around the edges of the jar, gently shifting the food, so that any trapped air is released. After the air bubbles have been removed, more liquid may need to be added to the jar to ensure proper head space.

Wipe off the rims of the jars with a clean, damp cloth.

Screw on the lids, but not too tightly. Air needs to escape during processing.

Put filled glass jars on the rack in the canner. Add more boiling water or take out some as needed so that the water is at least 1 inch over the tops of the jars. (If you add more water, pour it between the jars, not directly on them, to prevent breakage.) Put the lid on the canner.

When the water in the canner reaches a rolling boil, begin timing. Boil gently and steadily for the recommended time, adjusting the heat and adding more boiling water as necessary.

Use a jar lifter to carefully remove the jars as soon as the processing time is up. Place the hot jars right-side up on a rack, dry towels, boards, or newspapers to prevent the jars from breaking on contact with a cold surface. Leave at least 1 inch of space between jars.

Do not tighten the lids.

Allow the jars to cool untouched for 12 to 14 hours.

Steps for Pressure Canner Method

Be sure to read your manufacturer's instructions on the use of your pressure canner.

Place 2 to 3 inches of water in the canner. It should be hot but not boiling when canning raw-packed food; hot or gently boiling for hot-packed foods.

Fill the jars as described in raw pack or hot pack methods on page 116.

Allow proper head space, remove air bubbles, wipe jar rims, and put on lids.

Process:

Set the jars of food on the rack in the canner so steam can flow around each jar. Fasten the canner lid so that no steam begins to escape except through the vent. Turn heat to high and watch until steam begins to escape from the vent. Let the steam escape steadily for 10 minutes.

Close the vent using a weight, valve, or screw, depending on the type of canner you have. If you have a weighted-gauge canner that has a weight of varying pressures, be sure you are using the correct pressure.

For a dial-gauge canner, let the pressure rise quickly to 8 pounds of pressure. Adjust the burner temperature down slightly and let the pressure continue to rise to the correct pressure. (If the burner were left on high, the pressure would be hard to regulate when the correct pressure is reached.) Start counting the processing time as soon as the pressure is reached.

For weighted-gauge canners, let the canner heat quickly at first and then adjust the heat down slightly until the weight begins to rock gently or "jiggle" two to three times per minute, depending on the type of canner you have. Start counting the processing time as soon as the weight does either of these.

Keep the pressure constant by regulating the heat under the canner. *Do not lower the pressure by opening the vent or lifting the weight.* Keep drafts from blowing on the canner to prevent lowering the temperature of the contents. Fluctuating pressure causes underprocessing and the loss of liquid from jars.

When the processing is completed, carefully remove the canner from the heat. If the canner is too heavy to lift, simply turn it off.

Let the pressure in the canner drop to zero. This will take 30 to 45 minutes in a standard heavy-walled canner and nearly an hour for a larger 22-quart canner.

Newer thin-walled canners depressurize more quickly. Do not rush the cooling by setting the canner in water or by running cold water over the canner. *Never lift the weight or open the vent to hasten the reduction in pressure.*

Older canners are depressurized when the gauge on a dial-gauge canner registers zero or when a gentle nudge to the weight on a weighted gauge canner does not produce steam or resistance. New canners are equipped with a safety lock. These canners are depressurized when the safety lock drops to normal position. When a canner is depressurized, open the vent or remove the weight. Wait two minutes and then open the canner.

Note: Sometimes safety locks that are located in the handle of a canner will stick. If a nudge to a canner weight shows that it is depressurized, remove the weight, wait two minutes and then run a knife blade between the handles to release the lock.

Unfasten the lid and tilt the far side up, so the steam escapes away from you. Do not leave the canner unopened, or the food inside could begin to spoil. Use a jar lifter to carefully remove the jars from the canner. Place the hot jars on a rack, dry towels, boards, or newspaper right-side up to prevent the jars from breaking on contact with a cold surface. Leave at least 1 inch of space between the jars.

Do not tighten the lids. Allow the jars to cool untouched for 12 to 24 hours.

Test the lids to make sure they are correctly sealed (see page 25). If a jar is not sealed, refrigerate it and use the unspoiled food within two to three days, reprocess the food within 24 hours at the original processing time (see page 118), or freeze it in a plastic freezer-proof container. If liquid has been lost from sealed jars do not open them to replace it; simply plan to use these jars first. The food may discolor but if the jars are sealed, the food is safe. The screw bands should be removed from the sealed jars to prevent them from rusting on. The screw bands should then be washed, dried, and stored for later use. Wash food residue from the jars and rinse. Label with contents, date, and lot number (if you canned more than one canner load that day). It is important to write down the lot number so that if one jar spoils, you can identify the others from that canner load. Store in a clean, cool, dark, dry place. The best temperature is between 50 and 70°F. Avoid storing canned foods in a warm place near hot pipes, a range or a furnace, or in direct sunlight. They lose quality in a few weeks or months, depending on the temperature and may even spoil. Keep canned goods dry. Dampness may corrode metal lids and cause leakage so food will spoil. For best quality, use canned foods within one year.

Do not taste or use canned food that shows any sign of spoilage! Look closely at all jars before opening them. A bulging lid or leaking jar is a sign of spoilage. When you open the jar, look for other signs such as spurting liquid, an off-odor, or mold. Spoiled canned foods should be discarded in a place where they will not be eaten by humans or pets. If you have any questions concerning food safety, do not hesitate to contact your local extension service agent.

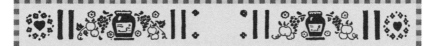

SOME VEGETABLE RECIPES

By Elizabeth Lloyd Gilbert
July 1913

Vegetables can be canned just as easily as fruits. All that is necessary is that the same care be exercised in the boiling of cans and lids, that new lids are always used, and that the vegetables be in perfect condition. The tomato is perhaps the most valuable and yet is regarded by many as hard to can. The following methods have been used in our family for years, with no cans spoiling. I use glass cans and store all vegetables and fruit in the cellar, where the light does not strike them directly.

❦ Whole or Halved Tomatoes, Packed Raw Without Liquid

Wash tomatoes. Dip in boiling water for 30 to 60 seconds or until skins split, then dip in cold water. Slip off skins and remove cores. Leave whole or halve. Add 1 tbsp. bottled lemon juice per pint to the jars and ½ tsp. of salt per quart, if desired. Fill jars with raw tomatoes; press pieces in until spaces between them fill with juice. Leave ½ inch of head space. Wipe jar rims. Adjust lids and process:

Boiling water bath, pints or quarts: 85 minutes

Dial-gauge pressure canner at 11 pounds pressure or weighted-gauge pressure canner at 10 pounds pressure, pints or quarts: 25 minutes
—*Adapted from Clemson University Extension Service website*

❧ Whole or Halved Tomatoes Packed in Water

Wash tomatoes. Dip in boiling water for 30 to 60 seconds or until skins split; then dip in cold water. Slip off skins and remove cores. Leave whole or halve. Add 1 tbsp. bottled lemon juice per pint to jars.

Hot pack: Add enough water to cover the tomatoes and boil them gently for 5 minutes. Fill jars with hot tomatoes or with raw peeled tomatoes. Add the hot cooking liquid to the hot pack, leaving ½ inch of head space. Adjust lids and process (see below).

Raw pack: Heat water for packing tomatoes to a boil. Add 1 tsp. salt to each quart, ½ tsp. to each pint jar, if desired. Pack prepared tomatoes in hot jars, leaving ½ inch of head space. Fill hot jars to ½ inch from top with boiling water. Adjust lids and process:

Boiling water bath, pints: 40 minutes; quarts: 45 minutes

Dial-gauge pressure canner at 11 pounds pressure, or weighted-gauge pressure canner at 10 pounds pressure, pints or quarts: 10 minutes
—*Adapted from Clemson University Extension Service website*

❧ Crushed Tomatoes with No Added Liquid

Wash tomatoes and dip in boiling water for 30 to 60 seconds or until skins split. Then dip in cold water, slip off skins, and remove cores. Trim off any bruised or discolored portions and quarter. Heat ⅙ of the quarters quickly in a large pot, crushing them with a wooden mallet or spoon as they are added. This will draw out the juice. Continue heating the tomatoes, stirring to prevent burning. Once the tomatoes are boiling, gradually add remaining quartered tomatoes, stirring constantly. These remaining tomatoes do not need to be crushed. They will soften with heating and stirring. Continue until all tomatoes are added. Then boil gently 5 minutes. Add 1 tbsp. bottled lemon juice per pint to jars (2 tbsp. per quart) and ½ tsp. salt per pint, if desired. Fill jars immediately with hot tomatoes, leaving ½ inch of head space. Wipe jar rims. Adjust lids and process:

Boiling water bath, pints: 35 minutes; quarts: 45 minutes

Dial-gauge pressure canner at 11 pounds pressure or weighted-gauge pressure canner at 10 pounds pressure, pints or quarts: 15 minutes
—*Adapted from Clemson University Extension Service website*

❦ Tomatoes the Old-Fashioned Way
July 1913

We prefer the tomatoes that are to be used in soups canned in the "old-fashioned" way. And I accidentally discovered that those barely ripe are much more delicately flavored. Take them directly from the market or garden; wash, scald, peel. Cut them into small pieces; salt as though you were readying them for the table. To every gallon of tomatoes add 1 tsp. baking soda; use no water. Cook, allowing them to come to the boil 3 times in succession, skimming each time. Then let simmer 20 minutes. Add bottled lemon juice or citric acid, and salt, following instructions on page 114; pack hot in hot, sterile jars or freezer-proof containers and store immediately in refrigerator or freezer.
—*Adapted from the NCHFP website*

❦ Tomatoes with the New Method
July 1913

This is the "whole tomato" recipe. Select large ripe tomatoes. Prepare as for old-fashioned tomatoes, but do not cut the fruit. Place in baking pans, sprinkle with salt to taste, and bake slowly at 300°F until almost covered with juice, about 30 minutes to 1 hour; the tomatoes should remain firm. Lift the tomatoes carefully into hot, sterile jars. Pour juice from baking pan and add bottled lemon juice or citric acid according to instructions on page 114; bring to the boiling point and pour over tomatoes. Seal jars and store immediately in refrigerator [jars] or freezer [plastic].

If this method is followed, the tomatoes may be served exactly as you do fresh ones, and the juice [can be] used for soups. Sliced tomatoes with salad dressing are a delightful surprise for the country Christmas dinner. They may be stuffed and baked, requiring but 10 minutes in a hot oven.

❦ Tomato Sauce for Spaghetti
February 1929

This sauce may be used for seasoning meats or soups or for macaroni and spaghetti dishes.

30 lbs. tomatoes, washed, skins and
    cores removed
1 c. onion, chopped
1 c. chopped celery
4 tbsp. minced parsley
2 tbsp. salt
4 tbsp. sugar
2 bay leaves
¼ c. olive oil

Cook tomatoes 20 minutes, uncovered, then put through a food mill to remove seeds. Chop onions and soften in a little oil with celery in a kettle over a low flame. Add tomatoes, parsley, and seasonings, bring to a boil, then cook at moderate heat until reduced by one-half. Remove bay leaves and pack in hot, clean jars, adding bottled lemon juice following instructions on pg. 114. Leave 1 inch of headspace. Seal and process.

Dial-gauge canner at 11 pounds pressure or a weighted-gauge pressure canner at 10 pounds pressure. Pints: 20 minutes; quarts: 25 minutes
—*Adapted from the NCHFP website*

❦ Seasoned Tomato Sauce
Makes about 5 half-pint jars

10 lbs. tomatoes, peeled, cored, and chopped
3 medium onions, finely chopped
3 cloves garlic, minced
1½ tsp. oregano
2 bay leaves
1 tsp. salt
1 tsp. black pepper
½ tsp. crushed red pepper
1 tsp. sugar

Place all ingredients in a large saucepan. Bring to a boil. Simmer 2 hours, stirring occasionally. Press mixture through a food mill and discard seeds. Cook mixture until thick over medium-high heat, stirring frequently. Add bottled lemon juice to jars in the following ratio: 1 tbsp. per pint. Pour hot sauce into hot, clean pint jars, leaving ½ inch head space. Wipe jar rims. Adjust lids and process 35 minutes in a boiling water canner, or 15 minutes in a dial-gauge canner at 11 pounds pressure or a weighted-gauge pressure canner at 10 pounds pressure.
—*Adapted from the Clemson University Extension Service website*

🦋 Tomatoes with Okra or Zucchini

About 12 lbs. of tomatoes and 4 lbs. of okra or zucchini are needed to make 7 qt., and about 7 lbs. of tomatoes and 2½ lbs. of okra or zucchini to make 9 pints.

Wash tomatoes and okra or zucchini. Dip tomatoes in boiling water 30 to 60 seconds or until skins split. Then dip in cold water, slip off skins, remove cores, and quarter. Trim stems from okra and slice into 1-inch pieces or leave whole. Slice or cube zucchini if used. You may also add four or five pearl onions or two ¼-inch-thick onion slices to each jar. Bring tomatoes to a boil and simmer 10 minutes. Add okra or zucchini and boil gently 5 minutes more. Add 1 tsp. of salt per quart to the jars, if desired, and bottled lemon juice following the directions on page 114. Fill hot jars with hot mixture, leaving 1-inch head space. Remove air bubbles. Wipe jar rims. Adjust lids and process:

Dial-gauge pressure canner at 11 pounds pressure or in a weighted-gauge pressure canner at 10 pounds pressure. Pints: 30 minutes; quarts: 35 minutes
—Adapted from NCHFP website

🦋 Preserved Tomatoes
September 1913

A classic recipe, revised to a refrigerator pickle. Make what you can eat within a week.

Select firm, perfectly ripe tomatoes, scald, peel, and quarter. Weigh and allow equal parts sugar. Place in nonreactive bowl overnight in refrigerator with sugar between layers of tomatoes. In the morning place in a kettle with 1 c. vinegar per gallon of tomatoes and 2 tbsp. whole cloves. Boil until quite thick. Pack hot in hot, sterile jars, and store immediately in the refrigerator, using up within a week. This is a fine preserve and equals any made of fruit.

❦ Stewed Tomatoes

2 qt. chopped tomatoes
¼ c. chopped green peppers
¼ c. chopped onions
2 tsp. celery salt
2 tsp. sugar
¼ tsp. salt

Combine ingredients, cover, and cook 10 minutes, stirring often.
Pour hot into hot, clean pint or quart jars, leaving ½ inch of head
space. Remove air bubbles with a bubble freer, wipe jar rims, adjust
lids, and process.

Dial-gauge pressure canner at 11 pounds pressure or in a weighted-
gauge pressure canner at 10 pounds pressure. Pints: 15 minutes;
quarts: 20 minutes
—*Adapted from the Clemson University Extension Service website*

❦ Tomato Catsup I

24 lbs. ripe tomatoes
3 c. onions, chopped
¾ tsp. cayenne
4 tsp. whole cloves
2 sticks cinnamon, crushed into small pieces under a knife handle
1½ tsp. whole allspice
2 tbsp. celery seeds
3 c. vinegar (5 percent acidity)
1½ c. sugar
¼ c. canning or pickling salt

Wash tomatoes. Dip in boiling water for 30 to 60 seconds or until skins split. Then dip in cold water, slip off skins, and remove cores. Quarter tomatoes and place in a 4-gallon pot. Add onions. Bring to boil and simmer 20 minutes, uncovered. Combine spices in a spice bag. Place spices in a spice bag and vinegar in a 2-quart saucepan. Bring to boil. Cover, turn off heat, and let stand for 20 minutes. Remove spice bag from the vinegar and add the vinegar to the tomato mixture. Boil about 30 minutes. Press boiled mixture through a food mill or sieve. Return to the pot. Add sugar and salt and boil gently, stirring frequently until volume is reduced by one-half or until mixture rounds up on spoon without separation. Pour into clean, hot pint jars, leaving ⅛ inch of head space. Wipe jar rims. Adjust lids. Process 15 minutes in a boiling water canner.
—*Adapted from the NCHFP website*

❧ Tomato Catsup II
September 1913

24 lbs. tomatoes, strained
1 tbsp. peppercorns
1 tbsp. whole cloves
2 sticks cinnamon
2 tbsp. whole allspice
2⅔ pints vinegar (5 percent acidity)
1½ c. sugar
¼ c. canning or pickling salt

Follow directions for Tomato Catsup I, above.
—*Adapted from the NCHFP website*

❦ Tomato Catsup III
June 1917

4 lbs. ripe tomatoes
3 c. onion, chopped
1 tsp. red pepper
3 bay leaves
1 lemon
1 tsp. white pepper
1 tsp. black pepper
2 tsp. mustard powder
3 c. vinegar (5 percent acidity)
¼ c. canning or pickling salt
1½ c. sugar

Follow directions for Tomato Catsup I, above, placing whole spices in spice bag and adding powdered spices and lemon as is.
—*Adapted from the NCHFP website*

❦ Spiced Tomatoes I
July 1913

These two recipes for spiced tomatoes create two pungent sauces, not unlike the above catsup recipes.

24 lbs. ripe tomatoes
1¼ c. brown sugar
4 tsp. whole cloves

4 tsp. whole allspice berries
2⅔ c. good vinegar (5 percent acidity)
¼ c. canning or pickling salt

Follow directions for preparing tomatoes from Tomato Catsup I, above. Add sugar, spices, and cinnamon, and cook and process according to directions in Tomato Catsup I.
—*Adapted from the NCHFP website*

❧ Spiced Tomatoes II

Using 24 lbs. tomatoes, ¼ c. canning salt, 2⅔ c. 5-percent vinegar, and 1¼ c. sugar, follow directions for Tomato Catsup I (above), spicing with 2 tsp. each whole cloves, allspice, peppercorns, and 4 sticks cinnamon.
—*Adapted from the NCHFP website*

❧ Tomato Juice
July 1938

Editor's note: In July of 1938 The Farmer's Wife *was gung-ho for canning tomato juice. This was still the era of the tomato juice cocktail: a small glass of the stuff to start off a meal, in place of another favorite appetizer of the era, half a grapefruit. Directions here are adapted from the NCHFP's website updates for preparation and processing.*

About 23 pounds is needed to make 7 quarts and 14 pounds to make 9 pints.

Wash tomatoes, remove stems, and cut in quarters directly into a large kettle. Crush, heat, and simmer 5 minutes. Press through a food mill or strainer to remove skins and seeds and then heat again to boiling. Add lemon juice and salt according to directions on page 114 (The Basics) to clean hot jars and fill with tomato juice. Seal and process in a boiling water canner: pints, 35 minutes, and quarts, 40 minutes. In a dial-gauge pressure canner at 11 pounds pressure or in a weighted-gauge pressure canner at 10 pounds pressure, pints or quarts: 15 minutes.

❧ Spiced Green Tomatoes

6 lbs. small, whole green tomatoes, such as plum tomatoes
9 c. sugar
1 pt. cider vinegar (5 percent acidity)

2 sticks cinnamon
1 tbsp. whole cloves
1 tbsp. whole allspice
1 tbsp. whole mace or ½ tbsp. ground

Wash, scald, and peel tomatoes. Make a syrup of the sugar, vinegar, and spices. Drop the tomatoes into the syrup and boil until they become clear. Pack into hot, clean pint jars, leaving ½ inch of head space. Strain syrup and pour over tomatoes with the syrup, again leaving ½ inch of head space. Remove air bubbles and adjust head space if needed. Wipe rims of jars with a dampened clean paper towel; seal and process 15 minutes in a boiling water bath.
—*Adapted from the NCHFP website*

FRUITLESS PRESERVES

Lulu G. Parker
August 1910
With fruit so high and scarce this summer, the thrifty housewife may well turn to the vegetable garden for the wherewithall to fill her preserve jars. These tomato preserves are not mere substitutes; anyone who has tried them knows they are exceedingly "good eating."

Editor's note: The Farmer's Wife made tomato jam in the late summer of 1910 and Green Tomato Jam in the autumn of 1913, and similar recipes dozens of times over the years. Below are the recipes, for which no contemporary processing times exist. They should be stored in the refrigerator for immediate use. Following them are two modern recipes, for Spiced Tomato Jam with Powdered Pectin and Tomato Marmalade, both appearing on the NCHFP website.

❦ Tomato Jam
August 1910

Peel and slice ripe tomatoes, put them with an equal weight of sugar, and boil an hour with 6 tbsp. bottled lemon juice per every 1½ lbs. tomatoes and an equal measure of water to fruit. Tie ginger enough to flavor to taste (about 1-inch slice per 1½ lbs.) in a thin muslin bag and add to the jam before it is done, about 30 minutes. When it passes the jelly test, remove the ginger and skim. Pack hot in hot, sterile jars and store immediately in refrigerator, using up within a week.

❦ Green Tomato Jam
September 1913

6 lbs. green tomatoes
4 lbs. sugar
1 c. water
2 oz. grated fresh ginger

Slice tomatoes thin, mix with remaining ingredients, and simmer slowly for 3 hours. Strain through a coarse strainer. Pack hot in hot, sterile jars, seal, and store immediately in refrigerator.

❧ Spiced Tomato Jam with Powdered Pectin

Makes about 5 half-pint jars

3 c. prepared firm, ripe tomatoes
(see method below; use
about 2¼ lbs.)
1½ tsp. grated lemon rind
½ tsp. allspice
½ tsp. cinnamon
¼ tsp. ground cloves
¼ c. bottled lemon juice
4½ c. sugar
1 box powdered pectin

To prepare tomatoes, wash, scald, peel, and chop. Place in saucepan and heat slowly to simmering, stirring constantly to prevent sticking. Cover and simmer 10 minutes, stirring occasionally. Measure 3 c. of the cooked tomatoes into a large saucepan. Add lemon rind, allspice, cinnamon, cloves, and lemon juice. Measure sugar and set aside. Stir powdered pectin into prepared tomatoes. Bring to a boil over high heat, stirring constantly. At once, stir in sugar. Stir and bring to a full rolling boil that cannot be stirred down. Then boil hard for 1 minute, stirring constantly. Remove from heat. Skim off foam. Pour hot jam into hot, sterilized half-pint jars, leaving ¼ inch of head space. Wipe rims of jars with a dampened, clean paper towel; adjust lids, process for 5 minutes in a boiling water canner.

—*Adapted from the NCHFP website*

❧ Tomato Marmalade
Makes about 9 half-pint jars

3 qt. ripe tomatoes
  (about 5½ pounds)
3 oranges
2 lemons
4 sticks cinnamon

6 whole allspice
1 tbsp. whole cloves
6 c. sugar
1 tsp. salt

Peel tomatoes and cut in small pieces. Drain. Slice oranges and lemons very thin, then quarter slices. Tie cinnamon, allspice, and cloves in a cheesecloth bag. Place tomatoes in large kettle. Add sugar and salt; stir until dissolved. Add oranges, lemons, and spice bag. Bring to a boil, stirring constantly. Continue to boil rapidly, stirring constantly, until thick and clear (about 50 minutes). Remove from heat; skim off foam. Fill hot marmalade into hot, sterilized half-pint jars, leaving ¼ inch of head space. Wipe rims of jars with a dampened, clean paper towel; adjust two-piece metal canning lids. Process 5 minutes in a boiling water bath.
—*Adapted from the NCHFP website*

A GOOD AROMA
MAKES GOOD SALES

By Mrs. E. B. K., Oregon
September 1933

When I was making my winter supply of chili sauce, the house got full of the aroma of boiling vinegar, spices, tomatoes, and green peppers. It smelled so good that I thought, "Why wouldn't that aroma sell the stuff on the market?"

So I made up an extra batch and filled 40 half-pint mayonnaise jars at the cost of one dollar and 50 cents, or about 4 cents a jar. Figuring the jars at 5 cents apiece brought the cost to 9 cents a jar. I struck off some labels on the typewriter and was ready for the experiment.

When Saturday morning came I loaded my supplies in the car and took off for the Public Market. The first thing I did after renting a stall was to hook up an electric plate and put on a half-cooked kettle of chili sauce. Soon the fumes were drifting all over the market and people began following them to their source. All I had to do to get 20 cents a jar was to let them have a sample. I was sold out before noon and counted my profits, which were close to 6 dollars, not bad in these times.

Later I hired a woman to do the manufacturing while I did the selling—from 3 to 8 dozen a day.

❦ Chili Sauce I
September 1910

8 c. canned diced tomatoes
1½ c. Serrano peppers, seeded and chopped
4 c. white vinegar (5 percent acidity)
2 tsp. canning or pickling salt
2 tbsp. whole mixed pickling spice in spice bag

Bring all ingredients to a boil. Lower heat and simmer 20 minutes. Press through foodmill, then return to boil for 15 minutes. Pack into clean, hot pint jars, leaving ¼ inch of head space. Process for 10 minutes.
—*Adapted from the NCHFP website*

❦ Chili Sauce II
June 1917

3 lbs. hot peppers, washed, trimmed, and sliced into rings
⅓ c. garlic, minced
4 c. onions, sliced
⅓ c. cilantro leaves, chopped
3 28-oz. cans diced tomatoes
3 c. cider vinegar (5 percent acidity)
2½ c. water

Bring all ingredients to a boil and boil 1 hour. Remove from heat and cool slightly. Puree in blender in batches, then return to boil.
Pack into hot, clean pint jars, leaving ½ inch of head space. Process for 10 minutes.
—*Adapted from the NCHFP website*

SOME "CANNY" IDEAS

June 1932

Make your garden fit your canning. A lot of homemakers know how much they want to can, but haven't got much idea as to the amount of garden space to give over to each vegetable to come out fairly even on their cans.

In the middle of summer they find themselves long on beans or short on peas, or the other way around.

Here is a table that gives you some idea of the number of cans you can get from given amounts of the raw product.

1 bushel windfall apples	20 qt.
1 bushel peaches	18 qt.
1 bushel pears	30 qt.
1 bushel plums	30 qt.
1 crate (16 qt.) blackberries	14 qt.
1 crate (16 qt.) strawberries	12 qt.
1 bushel tomatoes	16 qt.
1 bushel string beans	20 qt.
1 bushel corn	12 qt.
1 bushel peas	10 qt.
1 bushel spinach or greens	7 qt.
1 bushel small beets or carrots	16 qt.

Preserved Vegetables and Vegetable Products

The farmer's wife canned all manner of vegetables by the bushel—everything from corn and beans to greens and potatoes.

The Basics

Mostly, the farmer's wife canned vegetables in a boiling water bath, a method that back in 1939 was considered perfectly safe but is now known to be extremely dangerous, since it does not necessarily kill off the deadly *Clostridium botulinum* microorganism. If you plan to can vegetables, you MUST be prepared to process them in a pressure canner. All methods and recipes in this chapter (except for refrigerator recipes) have been adapted from or checked against tested recipes from the following sources to ensure that they follow the latest standards for using pressure canners, most notably, the preparation of the particular vegetable and amount of time it should be processed: NCHFP website, Clemson University Extension Service website, and University of Georgia Extension Service website.

[To process, follow directions on pages 118–120 for using a pressure canner.] Times are for altitudes of 0 to 1,000 feet. As always, use only high-quality, freshly picked produce in excellent condition. Pint and quart jars are standard, and a bubble freer is a useful implement for removing air bubbles from jars before sealing.

TABLE TALK: HOME CANNING OF VEGETABLES AND FRUIT

By Ellen Shafroth
April 1912

At the first suggestion of spring and the thought of the good things to come in the garden, we realize that we are somewhat tired of our winter diet. This is especially so if dry vegetables or those bought from the grocer have been the only supply of "green stuff" during the winter months. And at the appearance of that "best seller of the year"—which comes without cost—the seed catalog, we eagerly scan its inviting pages in making the selection of our garden. Given a moderate amount of ground, a few packages of seeds and a half hour of time each day, on the average, plenty of delicious green vegetables and fresh fruits of the smaller varieties may be had for the average family's use, and a goodly supply for canning and preserving for the winter months to follow.

In foreign countries, large amounts of canned goods, both fruits and vegetables, are put up at home as a matter of course, and we are fast reaching that stage in this country. The canning of fruit has been quite largely undertaken by us; vegetables have been considered a more difficult matter, but there is really nothing mysterious about them and we may soon expect that every family having even a small garden, and

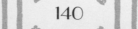

140

certainly every farmer with land a-plenty, will "put up" all the fruits and vegetables the family will require, and perhaps more. Many people are so situated that it is impossible to do this and in the supplying of their needs there is a large field for work, at a good profit, for the woman obliged to earn her own living, for the farmer's daughter, or for any other woman having a little spare time during the summer months, for many people will pay a trifle more than the price for store goods for the home-canned article.

On too many farms no attention is paid to the garden. Then men think they are too busy to plow and cultivate the garden plot and the women of the household often have plenty to do without this additional work; but once a garden is established nothing will induce the owners to give it up—if they are made of the right stuff.

A good garden and the canning of its products mean wholesome meals and consequently better health for the family, and a saving not only on doctor's bills but on the grocery bill as well. If the saving on the grocery bill alone is carefully considered, the intelligent farmer will realize that it really pays to take the time to plow and fertilize and cultivate that small garden plot for his family's use, and no one enjoys the luscious green corn, green peas, and string beans, the crisp cucumbers, lettuce and radishes, the sweet musk melons, more than the "boss of the ranch" himself.

Canning Vegetables
April 1925

In April 1925 *The Farmer's Wife* canned a whole bounty of vegetables and shared the techniques with its readers. Below are updated directions for preparing and processing these farmer's wife staples, using the hot-pack method and adapted from the NCHFP website, a division of the USDA. Remember: All vegetables must be processed in a pressure canner in order to be safe! A full-canner load is comprised of 7 quarts or 9 pints, and amounts needed for each vegetable are given along with the recipes. Add ½ tsp. canning salt per clean, hot pint jar and 1 tsp. salt per quart.

❧ Asparagus
You need about 24½ pounds of asparagus to make 7 quarts.

Wash tender, fresh, tightly tipped asparagus and trim off scales. Break off tough stems and wash again. Leave whole or break into 1-inch pieces. Blanch in boiling water for 3 minutes, then loosely pack into hot, clean jars, leaving 1 inch of head space. Add salt to jars then add boiling blanching water, again leaving 1 inch of head space. Seal and process: in a dial-gauge pressure canner at 11 pounds pressure or in a weighted-gauge pressure canner at 10 pounds pressure: 40 minutes.

❧ Beans, Green and Wax
You need about 14 pounds to make 7 quarts and 9 pounds to make 9 pints.

Wash fresh, tender beans and snap off ends. Blanch in boiling water for 5 minutes, then loosely pack into hot, clean jars, leaving 1 inch of head space. Add salt to jars then add boiling blanching water, again leaving 1 inch of head space. Seal and process: in a dial-gauge pressure canner at 11 pounds pressure or in a weighted-gauge pressure canner at 10 pounds pressure, pints: 20 minutes; quarts: 25 minutes.

❦ Beans, Lima

You will need about 28 pounds to make 7 quarts and 18 pounds to make 9 pints.

Shell fresh, well-filled pods and wash the beans. Cover with boiling water then return to a boil. Pack loosely into hot, clean jars, leaving 1 inch of head space. Add salt to jars then add boiling blanching water, again leaving 1 inch of head space. Seal and process: in a dial-gauge pressure canner at 11 pounds pressure or in a weighted-gauge pressure canner at 10 pounds pressure, pints: 40 minutes; quarts: 50 minutes.

❦ Beets

About 21 pounds of beets without their tops are needed to make 7 quarts, and 13½ pounds are needed to make 9 pints.

Trim small, fresh beets, leaving the roots and an inch of stem and scrub well. Blanch in boiling water 15 to 25 minutes til skins will slip off easily. Cool, remove skins, and cut off stems and roots. Cut into ½-inch cubes or slices. Add salt to hot, clean jars and pack with beets. Cover with boiling water, leaving 1 inch of head space. Seal and process: in a dial-gauge pressure canner at 11 pounds pressure or in a weighted-gauge pressure canner at 10 pounds pressure, pints: 30 minutes; quarts: 35 minutes.

❧ Carrots

You will need about 17½ pounds of carrots without their tops to make 7 quarts and 11 pounds to make 9 pints.

Wash, peel, and rewash fresh, tender carrots. Slice and blanch 5 minutes in boiling water. Add salt to jars then pack with carrots, leaving 1 inch of head space. Cover with boiling blanching water, again leaving 1 inch of head space. Seal and process: in a dial-gauge pressure canner at 11 pounds pressure or in a weighted-gauge pressure canner at 10 pounds pressure, pints: 25 minutes; quarts: 30 minutes.

❧ Corn

You will need about 31½ pounds of perfectly ripe corn still in the husk to make 7 quarts and 20 pounds to make 9 pints.

Husk ripe or slightly unripe ears of corn, remove silk, and wash. Blanch 3 minutes in boiling water, then cut off kernels about ¼ inch above the cob, taking care not to scrape the cob. To each quart of kernels add 1 quart of hot water, bring to a boil, and simmer 5 minutes. Add salt to jars then fill with the corn and water mixture, leaving 1 inch of head space. Seal and process: in a dial-gauge pressure canner at 11 pounds pressure or in a weighted-gauge pressure canner at 10 pounds pressure, pints: 55 minutes; quarts: 85 minutes.

❧ Cream-Style Corn

You will need about 20 pounds of corn still in the husk to make 9 pints. Do not can this in quarts!

Husk ripe or slightly unripe ears of corn, remove silk, and wash. Blanch 4 minutes in boiling water, then cut off kernels at their centers and scrape remaining corn from cob with a knife. To each quart of scraped-off corn add 2 c. boiling water and return to boil. Add salt to hot, clean jars then fill with corn mixture, leaving 1 inch of head space. Seal and process: in a dial-gauge pressure canner at 11 pounds pressure or in a weighted-gauge pressure canner at 10 pounds pressure, pints: 85 minutes.

❧ Greens: Spinach, Turnip, or Mustard

You will need about 28 pounds of greens to make 7 quarts and 18 pounds to make 9 pints.

Use very fresh greens in perfect condition. Wash small amounts of greens at a time, rinsing until completely free of dirt. Cut leaves from stems and midribs then place 1 lb. at a time in a basket or colander and steam 3 to 5 minutes until very wilted. Add salt to jars then pack loosely with greens, adding boiling water to cover and leaving 1 inch of head space. Seal and process: in a dial-gauge pressure canner at 11 pounds pressure or in a weighted-gauge pressure canner at 10 pounds pressure, pints: 70 minutes; quarts: 90 minutes.

❧ Okra

You will need about 11 pounds to make 7 quarts. Use tender pods in perfect condition. Wash okra and blanch in boiling water for 2 minutes. Drain. Add salt to jars, then pack loosely with okra, leaving 1 inch of head space. Cover with boiling blanching water, again leaving 1 inch of head space. Seal and process: in a dial-gauge pressure canner at 11 pounds pressure or in a weighted-gauge pressure canner at 10 pounds pressure, pints: 25 minutes; quarts: 40 minutes.

❧ Peas

You will need about 31½ pounds of peas in pods to make 7 quarts and about 20 pounds to make 9 pints.

Shell fresh, young, well-filled pea pods and wash peas. Blanch 2 minutes in boiling water. Add salt to jars then pack loosely with hot peas; cover with boiling blanching water, leaving 1 inch of head space. Seal and process: in a dial-gauge pressure canner at 11 pounds pressure or in a weighted-gauge pressure canner at 10 pounds pressure, pints or quarts: 40 minutes.

❦ Pumpkin

You need about 16 pounds to make 7 quarts and 10 pounds to make 9 pints.

Wash and peel fresh, small sugar pumpkins. Remove seeds and strings and cut in 1-inch cubes. Blanch for 2 minutes in boiling water. Add salt to clean, hot jars then pack with pumpkin cubes. DO NOT MASH OR PUREE. Cover with boiling blanching water, leaving 1 inch of head space. Seal and process: in a dial-gauge pressure canner at 11 pounds pressure or in a weighted-gauge pressure canner at 10 pounds pressure, pints: 55 minutes; quarts: 90 minutes.

❦ Sweet Potatoes

You need about 17½ pounds to make 7 quarts and 11 pounds to make 9 pints.

Wash small, mature, freshly harvested sweet potatoes and steam 15 to 20 minutes til somewhat soft. Remove skins and cut into bite-sized pieces. DO NOT MASH OR PUREE. Add salt to jars then pack with sweet potatoes, leaving 1 inch of head space. Pour over boiling water or syrup (see chart on page 83), again leaving 1 inch of head space. Seal and process: in a dial-gauge pressure canner at 11 pounds pressure or in a weighted-gauge pressure canner at 10 pounds pressure, pints: 65 minutes; quarts: 90 minutes.

❧ Peppers (Hot or Sweet)

About 9 pounds are needed to make 9 pints. Do not use quarts.

Select fresh, firm peppers in perfect condition. Wash and remove seeds and cores. Small peppers may be canned whole, large peppers may be cut in quarters. Cut a few slits in the skin of each pepper and blanch 2 minutes in boiling water. Allow to cool then peel; flatten whole peppers. Add salt to jars then pack loosely with peppers; cover with boiling water, leaving 1 inch of head space. Seal and process: in a dial-gauge pressure canner at 11 pounds pressure or in a weighted-gauge pressure canner at 10 pounds pressure, pints: 35 minutes.

❧ Succotash
March 1925

This recipe, a favorite of *The Farmer's Wife*, is adapted here from the NCHFP. It will yield 7 quarts of succotash.

3 qt. whole corn kernels, washed and cut as directed on page 144.
4 qt. shelled lima beans (prepared as directed on page 143)
2 qt. whole tomatoes (prepared as directed on page 121)

Combine vegetables in a large kettle with just enough water to cover. Boil 5 minutes. Add salt to hot, clean jars, then pack with vegetables and cooking liquid, leaving 1 inch of head space. Seal and process in a dial-gauge pressure canner at 11 pounds pressure or in a weighted-gauge pressure canner at 10 pounds pressure, quarts: 85 minutes.

❧ Mixed Vegetables
February 1929

The farmer's wife loved to can mixed vegetables. They added a touch of élan to her pantry. This mixture is adapted from the NCHFP. All vegetables should be prepared as directed on the preceding pages.

4 c. zucchini
6 c. sliced carrots
5 c. whole-kernel corn
6 c. green beans
6 c. lima beans
4 c. crushed tomatoes

Wash, trim, and cube zucchini. Prepare carrots, corn, green beans, lima beans, and tomatoes as directed on pages 142–144 and 121. Combine all vegetables in a large kettle, adding just enough water to cover. Boil 5 minutes. Add salt to hot, clean jars, then pack with vegetables and cooking liquid, leaving 1 inch of head space. Seal and process: in a dial-gauge pressure canner at 11 pounds pressure or in a weighted-gauge pressure canner at 10 pounds pressure, pints: 75 minutes; quarts: 90 minutes.

❧ I Can Vegetable Soup
August 1922

When fresh vegetables are plentiful, I can vegetable soup for winter use. We have been doing this for the past eight years, and find it advantageous to do so at a time when varieties of vegetables are plentiful and cheap. When winter comes, we can have a deliciously flavored soup that is not skimped in varieties of vegetables, some of which are not obtainable during that season. It has found favor with all our friends who have eaten it at our table and many of them are now canning it by the same recipe for home use.

We started canning vegetable soup as a method of utilizing surplus produce sometimes left over after supplying a retail trade. It was so well liked by the entire family that it has become one of our regularly canned products for home use each season.

Various combinations were tried at first, but the one always used now contains the following:

½ peck green beans (4 qt., or 16 c.)
12 ears sweet corn
12 medium-sized carrots
6 sweet mango peppers
6 red cayenne peppers
6 large onions
½ bushel ripe tomatoes

Editor's note: To update this recipe and make it safe for contemporary canning, it has been adapted from the NCHFP website and several vegetables have been removed for which no current processing recommendations exist: celery, cabbage and turnips. Proceed as follows:

Prepare beans, corn, and peppers as instructed on pages 142–144 and 147 and tomatoes as instructed for Crushed Tomatoes with No Added Liquid, on page 122. Select small, tender carrots, wash, peel, rewash, then slice and blanch in boiling water for 5 minutes. Select onions that are 1 inch in diameter or smaller, then wash, peel, and blanch in boiling water for 5 minutes. Combine all together and boil 5 minutes. DO NOT THICKEN or add rice or pasta. Season with salt to taste. Pack hot, clean pint or quart jars halfway with vegetables, then cover with remaining liquid, leaving 1 inch of head space. Seal and process: in a dial-gauge pressure canner at 11 pounds pressure or in a weighted-gauge pressure canner at 10 pounds pressure, pints: 60 minutes; quarts: 75 minutes.
—*Anna L. Mark*

PRODUCTS FROM NEW LANDS

June 1923

My garden was an inadequate square of newly broken land and my "orchard" one that Nature planted in the draws and along the streams.

I began with wild greens, picked in the morning, canned in the afternoon. I looked over and washed the greens, blanched in hot water, plunged into cold, cut in lengths, packed in hot jars and processed in a homemade water bath.

I got alfalfa greens first. They are very good if used young and tender; a day or two old makes them tough and bitter.

Lamb's quarter came next. It is delicious with salad dressing and hard-boiled eggs.

I found a few dandelions also, but they do not grow profusely on new land.

I canned some greens plain, with salt; to others, I added strips of bacon or bits of corned beef.

From my garden I canned beet greens, young beets, spinach, and rhubarb and made rhubarb jelly.

Later I canned peas and beans, but most of my canning was done in August as the garden stuff was ready and wild fruit ripe.

I made sweet, sour, mustard, olive oil, and dill pickles of cucumbers. I canned corn; corn and tomatoes; and tomatoes, corn, and beans.

I gathered a few buffalo berries for jelly and a quantity of wild plums and chokecherries. Part of those I canned and the rest I made into jelly.

Later I canned muskmelon, pickled cabbage, and onions, and made piccalilli, also canned tomatoes.

As cans became empty I refilled with sauerkraut, squash, and pumpkin or green tomato pickles.

I had new rubbers for all jars and new covers for most ... and did not lose a jar.

—Mrs. I. M., South Dakota

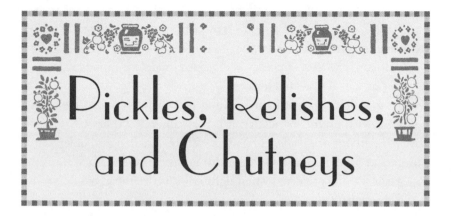

Pickles, Relishes, and Chutneys

As bland as the palate of the farmer's wife was when it came to soups, stews, and roasts, when she made pickles, relishes, and chutneys she much preferred those of a spicy, pungent nature. Her recipes for these products were well-on endless.

The Basics

All of the methods and recipes in this chapter (except recipes for refrigerator pickles) have been adapted and checked for safety against the following sources: the NCHFP website and the Clemson University Extension Service website.

Following is general information on fermented and pickled foods from the NCHFP website.

The many varieties of pickled and fermented foods are classified by ingredients and method of preparation. Regular dill pickles and sauerkraut are fermented and cured for about three weeks. Refrigerator dills are fermented for about one week. During curing, colors and flavors change and acidity increases. Fresh-pack or quick-process pickles are not fermented; some are brined several hours or overnight, then drained and covered with vinegar and seasonings. Fruit pickles

usually are prepared by heating fruit in a seasoned syrup acidified with either lemon juice or vinegar. Relishes are made from chopped fruits and vegetables that are cooked with seasonings and vinegar.

Be sure to remove and discard a ¹⁄₁₆-inch slice from the blossom end of fresh cucumbers. Blossoms may contain an enzyme that causes excessive softening of pickles.

Caution: The level of acidity in a pickled product is as important to its safety as it is to taste and texture.

Do not alter vinegar, food, or water proportions in a recipe or use a vinegar with unknown acidity. It is recommended that only vinegar with a 5 percent acidity level be used. White distilled and cider vinegars of 5 percent acidity (50 grain) are recommended. White vinegar is usually preferred when light color is desirable, as is the case with fruits and cauliflower.

Use only recipes with tested proportions of ingredients.

There must be a minimum, uniform level of acid throughout the mixed product to prevent the growth of *botulinum* bacteria.

Select fresh, firm fruits or vegetables free of spoilage. Measure or weigh amounts carefully, because the proportion of fresh food to other ingredients will affect flavor and, in many instances, safety.

Use canning or pickling salt. The noncaking material added to other salts may make the brine cloudy. Since flake salt varies in density, it is not recommended for making pickled and fermented foods.

White granulated and brown sugars are most often used. Corn syrup and honey, unless called for in reliable recipes, may produce undesirable flavors.

Pickle products are subject to spoilage from microorganisms, particularly yeasts and molds, as well as enzymes that may affect flavor, color, and texture. Processing the pickles in a boiling-water canner will prevent both of these problems. Standard canning jars and self-sealing lids are recommended. Processing times and procedures will vary according to food acidity and the size of food pieces.

For cucumber pickles, select firm cucumbers of the appropriate size: about 1½ inches for gherkins and 4 inches for dills. Use odd-shaped and more mature cucumbers for relishes and bread-and-butter style pickles, when they will be sliced or chopped.

For fermenting products, a 1-gallon container is needed for every 5 pounds of fresh vegetables. Therefore, a 5-gallon stone crock is the ideal size for fermenting about 25 pounds of fresh cabbage or cucumbers. Food-grade plastic and glass containers are excellent substitutes for stone crocks. Other 1- to 3-gallon nonfood-grade plastic containers may be used if lined inside with a clean food-grade plastic bag. Caution: Be certain that foods contact only food-grade plastics. Do not use garbage bags or trash liners. Fermenting sauerkraut in quart and half-gallon canning jars is an acceptable practice, but may result in more spoilage losses.

Cabbage and cucumbers must be kept 1 to 2 inches under brine while fermenting. After adding prepared vegetables and brine, insert a suitably sized dinner plate or glass pie plate inside the fermentation container. The plate must be slightly smaller than the container opening, yet large enough to cover most of the shredded cabbage or cucumbers. To keep the plate under the brine, weight it down with two to three sealed quart jars filled with water. Covering the container opening with a clean, heavy bath towel helps to prevent contamination from insects and molds while the vegetables are fermenting. Fine quality fermented vegetables are also obtained when the plate is weighted down with a very large clean, plastic bag filled with 3 quarts of water containing 4½ tbsp. of salt. Be sure to seal the plastic bag. Freezer bags sold for packaging turkeys are suitable for use with 5-gallon containers.

The fermentation container, plate, and jars must be washed in hot, sudsy water, and rinsed well with very hot water before use.

All pickle products may be processed in a boiling water canner. See detailed instructions on pages 21–25 (jelly chapter), but follow specific recipe instructions in this chapter for processing times.

CORA PICKLE'S PICKLES

By Miriam J. Williams
September 1938

The fact that her name was Cora Pickle before she was married probably had little to do with Mrs. Albert Wilson's success in making and marketing pickles from her own farm home and her husband's store near Clarksville, Texas.

But when she was quite young she was made sick on poor pickles and decided to learn to make good ones.

She made a beginning with 46 pounds of brined cucumbers in 1934. Last fall she and her husband brined 3,000 pounds of cucumbers and 350 pounds of white pickling onions. That her results are successful we realized fully when an attractive jar of Orange Ring Pickles came to the Country Kitchen—crisp slices of pickled cucumber with orange rind centers giving them a most intriguing spicy flavor. So fast has the Wilsons' fame spread that they have shipped pickles to no [fewer] than ten states.

Mrs. Wilson does not use alum to make her pickles crisp, but rather depends upon careful curing and gradual concentration of syrup during the sweetening process, which sometimes requires as long as five weeks. Only the best quality vinegar is used, an important factor in Mrs. Wilson's opinion.

When pickles have been canned for 10 days or two weeks, she opens a test jar or two, and if satisfactory in every way, into the store they go for sale. Small jars of from 6 to 11 ounces each, depending on the kind, sell at the store for 15 cents, 20 ½-ounce jars of sours and dills for 20 cents, and the same size of sweets or chow-chow for 25 cents. Their label, designed by Mrs. Wilson, is registered at the county courthouse.

Cucumber Pickles

❧ Bread and Butter Pickles

August 1930

6 lbs. pickling cucumbers
    4 to 5 inches long
8 c. onion, thinly sliced
½ c. canning or pickling salt
4 c. vinegar at 5 percent acidity
4½ c. sugar
2 tbsp. mustard seed
1½ tbsp. celery seed
1 tbsp. ground turmeric
3 tsp. ground ginger

Wash cucumber and cut in slices (USDA recommends 3⁄16 inch), discarding blossom ends. Mix cucumbers with onions and salt in a large bowl, covering with 2 inches of ice. Let stand in refrigerator 3 hours, adding more ice as ice in bowl melts. Combine sugar, vinegar, and spices in a large kettle and bring to a boil; boil 10 minutes then add drained vegetables. Slowly reheat to boiling then pack hot into hot, clean pint or quart jars, leaving ½ inch of head space, making sure vegetables are well-covered with syrup. Seal and process 10 minutes in a boiling water bath. Ideal pickle flavor develops after 4 to 5 weeks in jars.
—*Adapted from the NCHFP website*

❧ Quick Dill Pickles

8 lbs. pickling cucumbers,
    3 to 5 inches long
2 gallons plus 2 qt. water
1¼ c. canning or pickling salt
1½ qt. vinegar at 5
    percent acidity
¼ c. sugar
2 tbsp. mixed whole
    pickling spice
3 tbsp. whole mustard seed
4¼ tbsp. dill seed

Wash cucumbers and cut off blossom end; trim stem to ¼ inch. Dissolve ¾ c. salt in 2 gallons of water. Pour over cucumbers according to directions in Basics and let stand 12 hours. Drain. Combine vinegar with ½ c. salt, sugar, and 2 qt. water. Add pickling spice in spice bag and bring to a boil. Pack clean, hot pint jars with cucumbers; add 1 tsp. mustard seed and 1½ tsp. dill seed to each jar. Pour over boiling syrup, leaving ½ inch of head space. Seal and process 10 minutes in a boiling water bath.
—*Adapted from the NCHFP website*

❦ Quick Sour Pickles

25 medium-size pickling cucumbers
½ gallon cider vinegar at 5 percent acidity
2 c. water
½ c. salt
½ c. sugar
½ c. mustard seed

Wash cucumbers and slice off blossom ends; trim stem to ¼ inch. Slice cucumbers lengthwise and pack into clean, hot pint jars, leaving ½ inch of head space. Mix remaining ingredients in a large kettle and bring to a boil. Pour boiling syrup over pickles, leaving ½ inch of head space. Remove air bubbles, seal, and process 10 minutes in a boiling water bath.
—*Adapted from Clemson University Extension Service Website*

❦ Quick Sweet Pickles

8 lbs. pickling cucumbers,
    3 to 4 inches long
⅓ c. canning or pickling salt
4½ c. sugar
ice to cover

3½ c. vinegar at 5 percent acidity
2 tsp. celery seed
1 tbsp. whole allspice
2 tbsp. mustard seed

Wash cucumbers and slice off blossom ends; trim stem to ¼ inch. Slice cucumbers and cover with salt in a large bowl. Cover with 2 inches of ice and refrigerate 3 hours, adding more ice as ice in bowl melts. Bring remaining ingredients to a boil in a large kettle. Add drained cucumbers and bring *slowly* to a boil again, stirring to heat evenly. Pack into hot, sterile pint jars, leaving ½ inch of head space; pour over boiling syrup, leaving ½ inch of head space. Seal and process 5 minutes in a boiling water bath.
—*Adapted from the NCHFP website*

❦ Ripe Cucumber Pickles
September 1925

Many housekeepers consider ripe cucumbers good for nothing. If properly treated, they make a most delicious sweet pickle, well worth the small amount of trouble required to prepare it. A small quantity of this sweet cucumber pickle chopped fine will add an unusual and delicious flavor to almost any vegetable salad. Remember to store this favorite *Farmer's Wife* pickle in the refrigerator.

First, wash and pare the selected pickling cucumbers. Cut open lengthwise and remove seeds and inner fibers. Cut into slender strips, sprinkle with canning or pickling salt, and let stand 24 hours or at least overnight. Drain and cover with fresh water. Put over the fire and boil until tender and soft enough to be easily cut through with a spoon. Drain dry. Put in an earthen jar and cover with hot, spiced vinegar, prepared in these proportions:

1 qt. 5 percent cider vinegar
1½ lbs. sugar
1 tsp. allspice
1 tsp. cloves
½ tsp. paprika
2 tsp. cinnamon

Tie spices into muslin bag, then boil in vinegar and sugar mixture for 10 or 15 minutes. Remove spice bag and pour vinegar over prepared cucumbers. They should be well covered with liquid. Cover jar and set in cool place. Let stand two or three days, then drain off vinegar and heat again with same spice bag. When it has boiled freely for a minute or two, pour again over pickles. Let stand again two or three days then reheat to boiling and put hot into hot, sterile pint jars and seal. Store immediately in refrigerator.

❦ Ripe Cucumber Rings
August 1912

A *Farmer's Wife* favorite that's stored in the refrigerator.

Select large yellow cucumbers. Pare them and cut in slices ½ inch thick. Soak overnight in salt water (¼ c. salt to 1 qt. water). Drain, remove soft centers, and cook in clear water 20 minutes. Drain again and add to sweet pickle vinegar:

2 lbs. white sugar
2 c. vinegar
¼ tsp. cinnamon oil (available at canning supply stores)
⅛ tsp. clove oil (available at canning supply stores)
Mix sugar and vinegar and bring to a boil. Add cinnamon
    and clove oils.

Cook cucumbers in sweet pickle vinegar til translucent. Pour hot into hot, sterile pint jars; seal and store immediately in refrigerator.
—*Home Economics Extension, Cornell University*

❦ French Pickles
October 1927

Dear *Farmer's Wife:* I am sending you my favorite pickle recipe. I hope it will be liked.
—*Mrs. F. A. T., New York*

6 medium onions, chopped fine
½ c. canning or pickling salt
8 qt. large pickling cucumbers, peeled, seeded, and chopped
vinegar
3 lbs. brown sugar

(continued on next page)

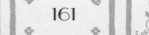

¼ lb. white mustard seed
¼ tsp. cayenne pepper
3 tbsp. ground cinnamon

Mix onions, salt, and cucumbers together and let stand overnight. In the morning drain and cook 15 minutes in equal parts 5 percent vinegar and water, enough to thoroughly cover (about 1 qt. each), drain again, then add vinegar to cover (about 2 qt.), add brown sugar, white mustard seed, cayenne pepper, and ground cinnamon. Cook until tender and seal at once in hot, sterile pint jars. Store immediately in refrigerator.

❧ J. Fenimore Cooper Pickles ❄

September 1924

½ c. canning or pickling salt
3 qt. pickling cucumbers, sliced as for table
3 large onions, slice or chopped
3 sweet peppers, sliced or chopped

Sprinkle ½ c. canning or pickling salt between layers of this mixture in a crock or nonreactive bowl. Let stand 3 hours. Drain. Mix the following ingredients:

1 qt. 5 percent vinegar
1 c. brown sugar
1 tbsp. yellow mustard seed
1 tbsp. celery seed
½ tbsp. turmeric

Bring to a boil and pour over vegetables in hot, sterile pint jars. Seal and store immediately in refrigerator.

❧ Olive Oil Pickles

August 1930

50 pickling cucumbers
6 large onions
½ c. canning or pickling salt
1 qt. water
1 qt. 5 percent vinegar
4 c. sugar
1 tsp. mustard seed
1 tsp. celery seed
1 tsp. ground black pepper
1 tbsp. olive oil

Slice onions and cucumbers and let stand in a solution of salt water (½ c. canning or pickling salt to 1 qt. water) overnight. Drain, boil with remaining ingredients. Pack hot in hot, sterile pint jars. Seal and store immediately in refrigerator.

❧ Mustard Pickles

September 1926

1 pt. small whole pickling cucumbers, no longer than 2½ inches
1 pt. sliced pickling cucumbers
1 pt. small whole onions
1 c. string beans, in 1-inch lengths
3 sweet green peppers, chopped
3 sweet red peppers, chopped
1 pt. cauliflower, in florets
¾ c. flour
1 c. brown sugar

(continued on next page)

3 tbsp. powdered mustard
½ tbsp. turmeric
I tsp. celery seed, crushed
I qt. 5 percent vinegar, heated to just below a boil

Cut vegetables before measuring. Put them in brine overnight
(see page 155) then freshen in clear water for 2 hours. Drain. Let
stand in a liquor of half 5 percent vinegar and half water for 15
minutes, then scald in same liquor. Drain vegetables thoroughly
and place in hot, sterile pint jars.

To make mustard dressing, rub all dry ingredients together until
smooth, slowly adding the I qt. hot vinegar, stirring to keep smooth.
Cook over double boiler, stirring carefully, until sauce thickens. Pour
over vegetables. Seal and store immediately in refrigerator.

❦ Pickle Gherkins
July 1910

Procure 7 lbs. small pickling cucumbers from I to I½ inches long and
slice off blossom ends, leaving ¼ inch of the stem attached. Pour over
them boiling salt water and let stand 8 hours. Drain; pour over 6 qt.
fresh water boiled with ¼ c. salt and let stand 8 hours. Drain and
prick all over with fork. Bring to a boil 3 c. vinegar at 5 percent acidity
with 3 c. sugar and spices tied in muslin bag: I oz. bruised ginger,
½ oz. peppercorns, ¼ oz. whole allspice, 4 cloves, 2 blades mace.
Pour over cucumbers and let stand 8 hours. Drain, discarding spice
bag but reserving syrup. Add to it 2 c. each of vinegar and sugar, boil
again. Pour over cucumbers and let stand 8 hours. Drain, reserving
syrup. Add to it I c. vinegar and 2 c. sugar, boil again. Pour over
cucumbers and let stand 8 hours. Drain, reserving syrup, and add to
it I c. sugar and 2 tsp. vanilla and boil again. Pack hot, sterile pint jars
with cucumbers and cover with hot syrup, leaving ½ inch of head
space. Seal and process 5 minutes in boiling water bath.
—Adapted from the NCHFP website

❧ Dill Pickles

July 1910

To this recipe, *The Farmer's Wife* originally added grape leaves (according to the USDA, grape leaves contain an enzyme that prevents softening but removing the blossom end from a cucumber has the same effect), bay leaves, green pepper, horseradish, and dill. This recipe provides a variation to this combination.

4 lbs. pickling cucumbers, 4 inches long
4 to 5 heads fresh dill, divided in half
2 tsp. whole mixed pickling spice, divided in half
½ c. canning or pickling salt
¼ c. vinegar at 5 percent acidity
8 c. water
2 dried red peppers

Wash cucumbers and slice off blossom ends; trim stem to ¼ inch. Place half the dill and half the spices at the bottom of a clean gallon container (see page 155). Add cucumbers and remaining dill and spices. Dissolve salt in vinegar and water and pour over cucumbers. Cover, weight, and cover with a clean towel. Store, maintaining a temperature of between 70°F and 75°F for 3 to 4 weeks, or at temperature of between 55°F and 65°F for 5 to 6 weeks. Check container several times a week and remove any surface scum or mold that develops. However, if pickles become soft, slimy, or foul-smelling, discard them.

Pour brine into a large kettle and bring slowly to a boil; lower heat and simmer 5 minutes. Filter through a coffee filter, then pour over pickles packed into hot, clean pint jars, leaving ½ inch of head space. Seal and process for 10 minutes in a boiling water bath.
—*Adapted from the NCHFP website*

❧ 14-Day Sweet Pickles

4 lbs. pickling cucumbers, 2 to 5 inches long
¾ c. canning or pickling salt
6 qt. water
4 c. vinegar at 5 percent acidity
5½ c. sugar
2 tsp. celery seed
2 tbsp. mixed pickling spice

Wash cucumbers, slice off blossom end; trim stem to ¼ inch. Bring to a boil ¼ c. salt and 2 qt. water in a large kettle and pour over cucumbers in 1-gallon container (see page 155). Cover, weight, and cover again with a clean towel. Maintain a temperature of about 70°F and let rest two days.

On the third day, drain cucumbers, rinse them, and re-sterilize cover and weight. Return cucumbers to container; bring to a boil ¼ c. salt and 2 qt. water in a large kettle and pour over cucumbers; replace cover, weight, and clean towel. Repeat this procedure on day 5. On day 7, drain cucumbers, rinse them, and re-sterilize container, cover, and weight. Slice cucumbers and return to container. Combine vinegar and 2 c. sugar in a large kettle, add spices in spice bag and bring to a boil. Pour over cucumbers, cover, weight, and cover with clean towel.

On each of the next six days follow this procedure: drain and reserve syrup and spice bag. Resterilize container, cover, and weight. Add an additional ½ c. sugar with spice bag and pour over cucumbers. Cover, weight, and cover with a clean towel.

On the 14th day, drain syrup into large kettle, add ½ c. sugar, and bring to a boil. Pack cucumbers into hot, sterilized pint jars and pour over boiling syrup (removing spice bag), leaving ½ inch of head space. Seal and process 5 minutes in a boiling water bath.
—*Adapted from the NCHFP website*

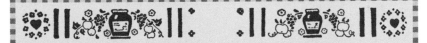

TEXTURE TRICKS IN PICKLES

By Miriam J. Williams
September 1935

When is a pickle a good pickle? Let an experienced judge of food products give the answer: "A pickle must have snap," she says. "It should add interest to a meal which already has enough bland, mild-flavored food. It must not be disagreeably sharp, for most people prefer a very slightly sweet taste along with the acid, nor should it be so heavily spiced that the mouth feels puckery. But as for texture, is there anything more sad than a soft, slippery pickle?"

Sometimes, the judge said, vegetables are cooked too long, as in mustard pickles or spiced fruit pickles. More often, the failure to get crispness is due to insufficient curing or perhaps poor vinegar. And remember, pickles need time. Almost all kinds need to stand in the jars to develop flavor before they are opened for use.

Causes of Pickle Troubles

Soft or slippery	Action on bacteria, due to too weak a brine or pickles exposed above brine
	Fermentation sets in because of weak vinegar solution
Poor color	Over-dark pickles may be caused by hard water
	Dark because of free spice
	Light or dull pickles may be due to scalding or poor-colored cucumbers
Hollow	Cucumbers not strictly fresh or poor quality
Shriveled	Too strong a salt or vinegar solution
	Too sweet a pickling syrup

Vegetable Pickles

❧ Beet Sweet Pickles
September 1911

7 lbs. beets, 2 to 2½ inches
        in diameter
4 c. cider vinegar at 5 percent acidity
2 c. brown sugar
1½ tsp. canning or pickling salt
2 c. water
2 cinnamon sticks
12 whole cloves
1 tsp. whole allspice

Trim off beet greens, leaving roots and 1 inch of stem. Wash and sort for size, cooking same-sizes together until tender, 25 to 30 minutes. Drain beets and cool. Peel and trim off roots and stems, slice ¼ inch thick. Combine vinegar, sugar, salt, and 2 c. new water in a large kettle with spices in a spice bag. Bring to a boil then add beets. Simmer 5 minutes, remove spice bag, and pack beets into clean, hot pint jars, leaving ½ inch of head space. Pour over hot syrup, leaving ½ inch of head space. Seal and process 30 minutes in a boiling water canner.
—Adapted from the NCHFP website

❧ Bean Pickles (Dilly Beans)
September 1911
Another almost-annual favorite of The Farmer's Wife.

4 lbs. green beans, 5 inches long
8 heads fresh dill
8 cloves garlic

½ c. canning or pickling salt
4 c. white vinegar at 5 percent acidity
4 c. water
1 tsp. red pepper flakes

Wash beans and trim ends to make each bean 4 inches long. Place
1 dill head and 1 clove garlic in each hot, sterile pint jar. Pack in beans
upright, leaving ½ inch of head space. Bring remaining ingredients to a
boil in a pot and pour over beans, again leaving ½ inch of head space.
Seal and process 5 minutes in a boiling water bath.
—*Adapted from the NCHFP website*

❧ Cabbage Pickle
September 1911

Take a large white cabbage and chop it fine, add 2 qt. 5 percent
cider vinegar, 1 tsp. each ground cloves, cinnamon, and mace in
a muslin bag, and 1 tbsp. canning or pickling salt. Boil all together
then pack hot in hot, sterile half-pint or pint jars, seal, and store
immediately in refrigerator.

❧ Spiced Carrots
September 1935

2 c. sugar
5½ c. vinegar of 5 percent acidity
1 c. water
2 tsp. canning or pickling salt
3½ lbs. carrots, washed, peeled, then washed again and cut in
    ½-inch rounds
1 tbsp. whole cloves
1 stick cinnamon

In a large kettle bring to a boil sugar, vinegar, water, and salt; boil 3 minutes, add carrots, and return to boil. Simmer 10 minutes with spices in spice bag, til carrots are partly cooked. Remove spice bag and fill clean, hot pint jars with carrots, leaving 1 inch of head space. Cover with hot pickling liquid, leaving ½ inch of head space. Remove air bubbles, seal, and process 15 minutes in a boiling water bath.
—*Adapted from the NCHFP website*

❦ Pickled Cauliflower
September 1914

12 c. cauliflower florets, cut in 1-inch pieces
4 tsp. canning or pickling salt
1 gallon water
4 c. white vinegar at 5 percent acidity
2 c. sugar
2 c. onion, thinly sliced
1 c. red bell pepper, diced
3 tbsp. mixed whole pickling spice
1 tsp. red pepper flakes

Wash cauliflower and boil for 3 minutes in salt water, at a ratio of 4 tsp. canning salt to 1 gallon of water. Drain and cool. Bring remaining ingredients (with pickling spice in a spice bag) to a boil in a saucepan, lower heat and simmer 5 minutes. Pack onion and pepper into clean, hot half-pint of pint jars, then cauliflower. Pour over hot syrup, leaving ½ inch of head space. Seal and process 10 minutes in a boiling water bath.
—*Adapted from the NCHFP website*

SPICE GIVES VARIETY

By Ina B. Rowe

August 1938

A cucumber is not the only garden product that can be converted into a pickle. Special treats in the form of sweet pickled fruits and vegetables will also find a ready welcome at the family dinner table.

Among the old standbys for sweet pickles are beets, watermelon rind, peaches, apples, pears, wax beans, carrots, apricots, cherries, dried prunes, and peppers. But we would not hesitate to lengthen the list if we believed the family's appetite could cope with more.

To pickle fresh vegetables, prepare as for cooking or canning, cook to tenderness, and drain thoroughly. To the drained vegetables add the following syrup, boiling hot:

❧ Sweet Pickling Syrup

1 c. 5 percent vinegar
2 c. sugar*
spices**

Bring the ingredients to a boil. Pour hot over drained vegetables and let stand for at least 48 hours in refrigerator, or until the desired strength has been developed. Reheat to boiling and pack hot into hot, sterile pint jars. Seal and store immediately in refrigerator.

*Brown or white sugar may be used, but white sugar gives a clearer color and, in this cook's opinion, a better flavor.

**Fresh whole spices give a better color than ground spices. They should be very fresh, as spices lose flavor from standing on the kitchen shelves.

❦ Pickled Mushrooms

September 1911

7 lbs. small, very fresh mushrooms no more than 1¼ inch in diameter, left whole
½ c. bottled lemon juice
2 c. olive oil
2½ c. white vinegar at 5 percent acidity
1 tbsp. canning or pickling salt
½ c. onion, diced
¼ c. pimiento, diced
2 cloves garlic, quartered
25 peppercorns

Wash mushrooms and trim stems to ¼ inch. Add to saucepan with lemon juice and water to cover; bring to a boil, lower heat, and simmer 5 minutes. Drain. Place oil, vinegar, salt, onion, and pimiento in saucepan and bring to a boil. Pack each clean, hot half-pint jar with ¼ clove garlic and 3 peppercorns, then pack in mushrooms. Cover with boiled mixture, leaving ½ inch of head space. Seal and process 20 minutes in a boiling water bath.
—*Adapted from the NCHFP website*

❦ Nasturtium Pickles ❄

August 1912
An unusual pickle, to be stored in the refrigerator. Use as a substitute for capers.

NASTURTIUM
SCARLET GLEAM HYBRID

PAGE'S SEEDS
GREENE, N. Y.

Gather the nasturtium seed pods when they are small and green, before the inner kernel has become hard. Remove the stems and let stand in salted water (use canning or pickling salt) overnight. Then freshen in cold water, pack in hot, sterilized half-pint jars and cover with boiling vinegar. Sweeten and spice the vinegar if you prefer. Seal and store immediately in refrigerator.

❧ Red Radish Pod Pickles
August 1912

Another unusual pickle, to be stored in the refrigerator.

Pick the seed pods while green and tender. Dissolve a cup of canning or pickling salt in 1 qt. of boiling water and pour it over the pods, cover tightly, and let stand overnight. Drain dry, pack in hot, sterilized half-pint jars, and cover with 5 percent vinegar that has been boiled with 1 c. sugar and a spice bag filled with 1 stick cinnamon and 1 tsp. mustard seed to season. Seal and store immediately in refrigerator.

❧ Pickled Onions
September 1911

8 c. white pearl onions, peeled
5½ c. white vinegar at 5 percent acidity
1 c. water
2 tsp. canning salt
2 c. sugar
8 tsp. mustard seed
4 tsp. celery seed

Blanch onions in boiling water and cool in cold water. Cut a 1/16-inch slice from the root end, remove peel, and cut a 1/16-inch slice from the other end. Bring vinegar, water, salt, and sugar to a boil in a large kettle for 3 minutes. Add onions and return to boil, then reduce heat and simmer 5 minutes until onions are half cooked. Put 2 tsp. mustard seed and 1 tsp. celery seed in each hot, clean pint jar then pack in hot onions, leaving 1 inch of headspace. Pour over hot pickling liquid, leaving ½ inch of headspace. Remove air bubbles, seal, and process 10 minutes in a boiling water bath.
—*Adapted from the NCHFP website*

❦ Pickled Peppers
September 1927

7 lbs. fresh, firm bell peppers
3½ c. sugar
3 c. vinegar at 5 percent acidity
3 c. water
9 cloves garlic, cut in half
4½ tsp. canning or pickling salt

Wash peppers and quarter, removing cores and seeds, and cut away blemishes; slice in strips. Boil sugar, vinegar, and water for 1 minute, then add peppers and return to boil. Place ½ clove garlic and ¼ tsp. salt in each hot, sterile half-pint jar, then pack in peppers. Pour over hot pickling liquid, leaving ½ inch of head space. Seal and process 5 minutes in a boiling water bath.
—*Adapted from the NCHFP website*

❦ Green Tomato Pickle I
September 1910

6 lbs. small, green plum tomatoes, left whole
9 c. brown sugar
1 pt. cider vinegar at 5 percent acidity
2 sticks cinnamon
1 tbsp. whole cloves
1 tbsp. whole allspice
½ tbsp. mustard seed
1 inch knob fresh ginger, peeled

Wash tomatoes then scald in boiling water and remove skins. Place spices in a spice bag and bring remaining ingredients to a boil in a large kettle, then add tomatoes; boil until they are clear. Pack hot into hot, clean pint jars, leaving ½ inch of head space. Strain syrup then pour over tomatoes, again leaving ½ inch of head space. Remove air bubbles, seal, and process 15 minutes in a boiling water bath.
—*Adapted from the NCHFP website*

❦ Green Tomato Pickle II
September 1911

¼ c. canning or pickling salt
10 lbs. green tomatoes, sliced
2 c. onion, peeled and sliced
3 c. brown sugar
4 c. cider vinegar at 5 percent acidity
2 cinnamon sticks
1 tbsp. whole cloves

Sprinkle salt over tomatoes and onions in a large bowl and let stand 6 hours. Drain. Heat sugar in vinegar in a large kettle until dissolved, then add spices in spice bag along with vegetables. If vegetables are not covered, add a small amount of water. Bring to a boil, lower heat, and simmer 30 minutes, stirring to prevent scorching, until tomatoes are transparent. Discard spice bag and pack tomatoes into clean, hot pint jars. Cover with syrup, leaving ½ inch of head space. Seal and process 10 minutes in a boiling water bath.
—*Adapted from the NCHFP website*

❦ Mixed Pickles I

September 1938

2 lbs. red and green sweet peppers
6 lbs. green tomatoes
2 lbs. onions
1 stalk celery
2 heads cauliflower
1 lb. cabbage
1 gallon 5 percent vinegar
8 c. sugar
3 hot peppers or 1½ tsp. ground red pepper
1 tsp. celery seed
2 tsp. yellow mustard seed
1 tsp. powdered mustard
1 whole nutmeg, grated
½ tsp. allspice
canning or pickling salt to taste

Wash and drain each of the vegetables and chop them, not too
fine, and mix all together except for the onions. Add vinegar,
sugar, hot peppers, and spices, tied in muslin bag. Bring to boil
and cook until almost tender, about 30 minutes, then add
onions. (After the mixture starts boiling it usually takes about 30
minutes.) Pack hot into hot, sterile half-pint or pint jars, seal, and
store immediately in refrigerator.

❦ Mixed Pickles II

4 lbs. pickling cucumbers 4 to 5 inches long, washed, blossom end
     discarded, and cut in 1-inch slices
2 lbs. small onions, peeled and quartered
ice to cover
5 c. white vinegar at 5 percent acidity

4 c. celery, chopped and cut in 1-inch pieces
2 c. carrots, peeled and cut in ½-inch pieces
2 c. red bell pepper, cut in ½-inch pieces
2 c. cauliflower florets
5 c. white vinegar at 5 percent acidity
¼ c. prepared mustard
½ c. canning or pickling salt
3½ c. sugar
3 tbsp. celery seed
2 tbsp. mustard seed
½ tsp. whole cloves
½ tsp. turmeric

Mix vegetables together in a large bowl and cover with 2 inches of ice. Refrigerate 3 hours, adding more ice as ice in bowl melts. Drain. Place spices in spice bag and combine remaining ingredients in a large kettle, stir to mix well, and bring to a boil. Add vegetables, cover, and slowly bring to a boil. Pack vegetables into hot, sterile pint jars, leaving ½ inch of head space, then pour over pickling solution, discarding spice bag, again leaving ½ inch of head space. Remove air bubbles, seal, and process 5 minutes in a boiling water canner.
—*Adapted from the NCHFP website*

❦ West India Pickles
October 1911

Chop fine 3 gallons green tomatoes and let drain overnight. Chop 1 small head cabbage, 4 peppers, 8 carrots, and 2 onions. Mix all together. Add 1 lb. brown sugar, 4 oz. mustard seed, 1 oz. celery seed, 1 tbsp. each cinnamon, cloves, and ginger, and 1½ c. canning or pickling salt. Cover well with good 5 percent vinegar and boil for 2 hours. Seal up in hot, sterile jars and store immediately in refrigerator.

MOTHER AND DAUGHTER, PARTNERS
Together They Earn Money Without Leaving the Farm Home

By Grace Viall Gray
June 1916

A new profession is open to all women who are fortunate enough to have gardens. You are wondering already what gardens can have to do with a bank account. You are saying, "But I can't sell garden stuff in my own town, for everyone has his own garden!" Of course everyone has and that is why you are going to make money. You are going to *can*, yes *can*, every bit of surplus fruits and vegetables that grows in your garden as well as your neighbors' gardens!

Now that I am very sure that I have your complete attention, I shall tell you how to go about it. . . .

Really, to be successful, in this new project or idea that I am putting before you, the mother and daughter must work side by side, as well as neighbor with neighbor. If the mothers and daughters in your community will band together on a cooperative plan, you can work wonders during the canning season.

Now is the time. Do not let another day pass before you form a Mother-Daughter Home Canning Club in your community. Then you can be enrolled at your college or at Washington and be recognized officially. In this way you may obtain all the help and information necessary for turning your garden into real money and get suggestions about the use of labels which will go on your jars and cans and give you a good market.

Just what are the Mother-Daughter Home Canning Clubs?

The mothers and daughters unite in an organization and call it a Mother-Daughter Club.

The daughters, to be members of this interesting club, must be ten to eighteen years of age. The mothers have no age limit attached to them.

The club-project interest is to be confined entirely to canning—canning of fruits, vegetables, soups, and meats for the first year. The Mother-Daughter team may choose its own method of getting vegetables and fruits to can. They may grow them in their own gardens or orchards or they may purchase the products for canning purposes. In this feature, the Mother-Daughter Club differs from the Tomato Clubs, where each member operates a tenth of an acre of land.

Every mother should want her daughter to strive to produce good products and exhibit her goods at the local and state fairs.

At nearly every state fair an exhibit of canned goods is arranged for by either the United States Department of Agriculture or the State Agricultural and Mechanical College. The entries are made by girl members of canning clubs.

To find a market, [a] government specialist says, "After the vegetables and fruit have been canned and the preserves and catsup made, an important part of the work remains and that is to find a good market for the product. Start out with the idea that there is a good market for your product and do not lack confidence in yourself to find it.

"The very best people are likely to want your products. ... Many housewives living in the city who leave home for the country during the summer months would gladly give you an order to can enough goods to last them all winter. Go to see all that you can, taking with you samples of your products put up in an attractive form."

In one county the merchants report that since women have gone "a-canning," their bills for canned goods have been reduced . . . but they are losing nothing because women are buying more things for their homes—labor saving devices or attractive pieces of furniture to make their homes more comfortable and homelike. You can be one of these women. Now is the time to begin. While the first impulse of interest is upon you, write to your state agent, talk with your daughters, your neighbors and their daughters, create enthusiasm, and follow up this enthusiasm with definite plans and decisive action.

❦ Spanish Pickles
June 1917

1 peck (8 qt.) green tomatoes (See page 174–175)
4 medium onions
1 c. canning or pickling salt
½ oz. each whole cloves, allspice berries, brown mustard seeds,
     peppercorns, placed in spice bag
2 c. brown sugar
4 green peppers
cider vinegar, at 5 percent acidity

Wash tomatoes and remove stem ends. Slice crosswise. Peel
onions and slice crosswise. Sprinkle alternate layers of tomatoes
and onion with salt and let stand 12 hours. Drain, place in pot with
remaining ingredients and enough vinegar to cover. Heat gradually
and boil slowly about half an hour. Pack hot into hot, sterile half-
pint or pint jars. Seal and store immediately in refrigerator.

PETER PIPER'S PICKLES

August 1932
Pickling season is here, and with it comes the urge to make a variety of
relishes and pickles for the winter months. And why? Because they add
a tang to many meals, they go well with meats, and most families crave
such foods. Best of all, they are not difficult to make.

Have you been guilty of discarding ripe cucumbers? If you have,
you'll be glad to know a delicious way to utilize them in cucumber rings,
or perhaps your family will prefer mustard pickles. The green meat part
of the watermelon is good, too, when made into watermelon pickles.

Fruit Pickles

❦ Sweet Apple Pickles
August 1912

Steam apples until they can be pierced with a fork then pop off
their peels; make a syrup using 4 lbs. of sugar to each quart of
vinegar and 3 tbsp. whole cloves and 8 cinnamon sticks placed in
a spice bag. When the apples are steamed, put them hot into hot,
sterile pint jars and pour boiling syrup over them, making sure to
cover them well with it. Seal and store immediately in refrigerator.
—*Mrs. Chas. Moffitt*

❦ Spiced Crabapples
September 1926

5 lbs. crabapples of uniform size
4½ c. apple cider vinegar at 5 percent
3¾ c. water
7½ c. sugar
4 tsp. whole cloves
4 sticks cinnamon
3-inch piece of ginger cut in 6 equal pieces

Remove petals from apples but leave stems attached. Wash and
then puncture skin 4 times with a toothpick. Mix vinegar, water, and
sugar in a large kettle and bring to a boil. Add spices in spice bag then,
using colander, submerge ⅓ apples at a time in syrup and leave in 2
minutes. Place cooked apples and spice bag in a clean 1-gallon crock
and pour over hot syrup. Cover and let stand overnight. Discard spice
bag, drain syrup into a large kettle, and reheat to boiling. Pack apples
into clean, hot pint jars and pour over hot syrup, leaving ½ inch of
head space. Seal and process 20 minutes in a boiling water bath.
—*Adapted from the NCHFP website*

❦ Melon Sweet Pickles

September 1911

The Farmer's Wife *was a big fan of the broadly titled muskmelon—really a whole species of melon that includes the cantaloupe. This recipe is very close in nature to pickles from the early twentieth century.*

2 medium cantaloupes, firm and green with no soft spots
4½ c. apples cider vinegar at 5 percent acidity
2 c. water
1 tsp. crushed red pepper
2 cinnamon sticks
2 tsp. ground cloves
1 tsp. ground ginger
1½c. sugar
1½ c. light brown sugar, packed

Wash melons and cut in halves to remove seeds. Peel and cut in 1-inch slices. Cut slices into 1-inch cubes. Weigh out 5 lbs. and place in a large glass bowl. Combine vinegar and water in a large pot and bring to a boil. Remove from heat and add spices in spice bag. Steep 5 minutes, stirring occasionally. Pour over melon, cover with plastic wrap, and refrigerate overnight. Drain vinegar solution into a large pot and bring to a boil. Add sugars and stir to dissolve. Add melon and return to a boil. Lower heat and simmer 1 to 1¼ hours, til melon is translucent. Strain out cantaloupe to a large bowl, keeping covered and warm. Return syrup to a boil and boil 5 minutes. Add melon again and return to a boil. Pack melon pieces into clean, hot pint jars, leaving 1 inch of head space. Pour over hot syrup, leaving ½ inch of head space. Remove air bubbles, seal, and process 15 minutes in a boiling water bath.

—*Adapted from the NCHFP website*

❧ Peaches and Peaches
August 1928

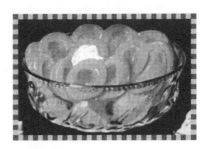

Peach pickles carry us to the next peach season—if I prepare enough! Cling peaches are my choice for pickling. To every 8 pounds of washed and pared fruit use 6¾ c. of sugar, 1 qt. 5 percent vinegar, and spices tied in a wee cheesecloth bag: 4 sticks cinnamon, 2 tbsp. whole cloves, and 1 tbsp. ground ginger.

Cover peaches with 2 qt. water and ½ tsp. ascorbic acid to prevent discoloring. Drain. Boil sugar and vinegar for 5 minutes. Add peaches and spice bag and cook until peaches are readily pierced with a toothpick, then remove from fire and let sit overnight. Return mixture to boil then fill hot, clean pint jars with peaches, leaving ½ inch of head space; then pour over syrup, leaving ½ inch of head space. Seal while piping hot. Process 20 minutes in a boiling water bath.
—*Gertrude Shockey*
—*Adapted from the Clemson University Extension Service website*

❧ Pickled Pears
September 1913 and June 1917

4 qt. small Seckel or other pickling pears, washed, peeled, blossom
    ends cut off, and put to soak in 2 qt. water and ½ tsp. ascorbic
    acid to prevent discoloration
8 c. brown sugar
4 c. cider vinegar at 5 percent acidity
2 c. water
8 cinnamon sticks
2 tbsp. whole cloves

Make a syrup by boiling together sugar, vinegar, water, and spices tied in spice bag. Lower heat and cover, then simmer 30 minutes. Drop in pears, bring to a boil, then lower heat and simmer, covered, until fruit is rich and clear—20 to 25 minutes. Pack hot into hot, clean pint jars with 1 stick of cinnamon from syrup per jar. Pour over hot syrup, leaving ½ inch of head space. Remove air bubbles, seal, and process 20 minutes in a boiling water bath.

—*Adapted from the NCHFP website*

❦ Watermelon Rind Pickles
June 1917 and August 1932

Pare rind and all pink edges from 6 lbs. watermelon. Cut into 1-inch squares. Cover with brine made by mixing ¾ c. canning or pickling salt with 3 qt. cold water. Add 2 trays of ice cubes. Let stand 3 to 4 hours. Drain; rinse in cold water. Cover with cold water and cook for about 10 minutes until fork tender (do not overcook). Drain. Combine 9 c. sugar, 3 c. 5 percent white vinegar, 3 c. water, and spice bag filled with 1 tbsp. whole cloves and 6 cinnamon sticks. Boil 5 minutes and pour syrup over the watermelon; add 1 thinly sliced lemon, seeds removed. Let stand overnight in the refrigerator. Heat watermelon in syrup to boiling and cook slowly 1 hour. Pack hot pickles loosely into clean, hot pint jars. To each jar, add a 1-inch piece of stick cinnamon from spice bag; cover with boiling syrup to ½ inch from top. Remove air bubbles. Seal and process 10 minutes in a boiling water bath.

—*Adapted from the NCHFP website*

Relishes

The Farmer's Wife devised an awful lot of relish recipes, few of which have a tested correlative. Recipes with a snowflake by the title should therefore be stored in the refrigerator and used up within a week to zip up homey comfort foods.

❦ Apple Relish I ❄

February 1927

1 pt. cider vinegar
2 c. brown sugar
1 c. water
1 tsp. ground cloves
½ tsp. paprika
2 tbsp. mustard seed
2 tbsp. celery seed
½ tsp. salt
1 tsp. ground cinnamon
1½ qt. apples
½ lb. seeded raisins
2 tbsp. onion, chopped
1 c. walnuts, chopped

Boil together vinegar, sugar, water and spices for 5 minutes. Add apples, raisins, and onion. Cook 1 hour at a brisk simmer. Five minutes before removing from fire, add nuts. Pack hot in hot, sterilized pint jars, seal, and store immediately in refrigerator.

❦ Apple Relish II

4 lbs. apples, peeled, cored, and thinly sliced, then soaked in 2 qt.
    water and ½ tsp. ascorbic acid to prevent discoloration
1¼ c. white vinegar at 5 percent acidity
1 c. sugar
½ c. light corn syrup
⅔ c. water
1½ tsp. whole cloves
2 sticks cinnamon, crushed
1 tsp. whole allspice

Combine all ingredients but apples in a large pot and bring to a boil.
Drain apples, add them to the syrup, and simmer 3 minutes. Return to
boil. Pack apples into hot, clean pint jars, leaving ½ inch of head space.
Pour over hot syrup, again leaving ½ inch of head space. Remove air
bubbles, seal, and process 10 minutes in a boiling water bath.
—*Adapted from the NCHFP website*

❦ Beet Relish I
August 1912

1 medium white onion
3 red peppers
1 qt. beets, parboiled about 20 minutes, then peeled and diced
2 tsp. salt
½ c. grated horseradish
2 c. vinegar
1 c. sugar

Chop onions and peppers and mix with beets. Combine
ingredients and cook until clear. Pack hot in hot, sterile pint jars,
seal, and store immediately in refrigerator.

❦ Beet Relish II
September 1938

1 qt. beets
3 sweet peppers
2 hot peppers
3 large onions
½ c. vinegar
1 c. sugar
½ c. water
3 large onions
2 hot peppers
1 tsp. salt
1 tsp. mixed pickling spice

Parboil beets about 20 minutes and peel. Then chop beets, peppers, and onions into long, thin strips. Boil the vinegar, sugar, water, and spice together about 10 minutes. Strain and pour syrup on the chopped vegetables. Cook until the onions and peppers are tender, 15 to 20 minutes, but be careful that you do not stir enough to make the beets mushy. Pack hot in hot, sterile pint jars, seal, and store immediately in refrigerator.

❦ Cabbage Relish
August 1912

1 qt. cabbage, chopped
1 qt. green tomatoes, chopped
1 c. red pepper, chopped
1 c. green pepper, chopped
2 c. white onion, chopped
1 c. sugar
5 tbsp. yellow mustard seed
1 tbsp. celery seed
½ tsp. turmeric
salt for brine (¼ c. salt to 1 qt. water)

Soak cabbage and tomatoes separately overnight in brine to cover. Drain off brine and combine all ingredients together. Let stand 2 hours. Simmer mixture until transparent. Pack hot in hot, sterile pint jars, seal, and store immediately in refrigerator.

❦ Celery Relish
October 1928

2 qt. celery, finely chopped
2 qt. cabbage, finely chopped
1 c. onion, finely chopped
½ c. salt
1 c. vinegar
2 tbsp. yellow mustard seed
2 tsp. celery seed
½ tsp. essence of cinnamon
½ tsp. essence of cloves
½ tsp. red pepper
8 bay leaves

Mix vegetables and salt together then drain for about 1 hour. Heat the vinegar and spices in a spice bag and add vegetables; bring back to a boil. Pack in hot, sterile pint jars. Seal and store immediately in refrigerator.

❧ Corn Relish

July 1913

20 ears fresh
    corn, to equal
    10 c. kernels
5 c. bell peppers, diced
2½ c. celery, diced
1¼ c. onions, diced
5 c. vinegar at
    5 percent acidity
1¾ c. brown sugar
2½ tbsp. canning or
    pickling salt
1¼ tsp. turmeric
2½ tbsp. dry ground
    yellow mustard seed
¼ c. flour
¼ c. water

Shuck corn, removing silk, and boil 5 minutes. Dip in cold water to cool then cut kernels from cob. In a large kettle bring to a boil celery, onions, vinegar, sugar, and salt and boil 5 minutes. Remove ½ c. of boiling liquid and mix with turmeric and mustard, then pour back into kettle, stirring to mix. Simmer 5 more minutes. Mix flour and water to make a paste and add to relish, stirring constantly til slightly thickened. Pack hot into hot, clean half-pint or pint jars, seal, and process 15 minutes in a boiling water bath.
—*Adapted from the NCHFP website*

❧ Wild Gooseberry Relish

August 1924

5 c. wild gooseberries
1½ lbs. raisins
1 medium onion
3 tbsp. salt
1 qt. vinegar
1 c. brown sugar
3 tbsp. ground mustard
3 tbsp. ground ginger
¼ tsp. cayenne pepper
1 tbsp. turmeric

Pick over, wash, and stem berries. Chop raisins and onion and add to gooseberries. Place in kettle, add remaining ingredients, bring slowly to a boil, simmer gently 45 minutes. Strain through a coarse sieve. Pack hot in hot, sterile pint jars. Seal and store immediately in refrigerator.

❧ Pepper Relish

August 1912

3 c. red bell peppers, finely chopped
3 c. green bell peppers, finely chopped
6 c. onions, finely chopped
6 c. vinegar at 5 percent acidity
1½ c. sugar
2 tbsp. canning or pickling salt

Combine all together in a large pot and boil gently til thick and reduced by one-half. Pack hot into hot, sterile half-pint or pint jars, leaving ½ inch of head space. Seal and process 5 minutes in a boiling water bath.
—*Adapted from the NCHFP website*

❦ Rhubarb Relish

June 1938

This relish is delicious with meats.

¼ lb. raisins, chopped
½ lb. dates, chopped
3 c. 5 percent vinegar
2 lbs. rhubarb
2 lbs. brown sugar
2 tsp. ground ginger
1 tbsp. canning or pickling salt
½ c. walnuts, chopped

Cover raisins and dates with vinegar in a nonreactive bowl and let stand about an hour. Wash rhubarb and cut in short lengths. Combine raisin, date, and vinegar mixture with all ingredients except nuts. Cook slowly until thick and clear—about 2 hours, stirring frequently. Add nuts, cook 10 minutes longer. Pack hot in hot, sterile pint jars, seal, and store immediately in refrigerator.
—*Mrs. D. C., Iowa*

❦ Green Tomato Relish

September 1913

10 lbs. small, hard green tomatoes
3 lbs. mixed green and red bell pepper, diced
2 lbs. onions, diced
½ c. canning or pickling salt
1 qt. water
4 c. sugar
1 qt. cider vinegar at 5 percent acidity
1 tsp. each cinnamon, cloves, and mace in spice bag
⅓ c. prepared yellow mustard
2 tbsp. cornstarch

Wash tomatoes, chop fine. Dissolve salt in water and pour over tomatoes in a large pot. Bring to a boil, lower heat, and simmer 5 minutes. Drain and return tomatoes to pot. Add remaining ingredients, stir, and bring to a boil; lower heat and simmer 5 more minutes. Discard spice bag and pack hot relish into hot, sterilized pint jars, leaving ½ inch of head space. Seal and process 5 minutes in a boiling water bath.
—*Adapted from the NCHFP website*

❧ Piccalilli
August 1932

6 c. green tomatoes, chopped
7½ c. green cabbage, chopped
3 c. red or green bell peppers, chopped
2¼ c. onions, chopped
½ c. canning or pickling salt
hot water
4½ c. vinegar at 5 percent acidity
3 c. brown sugar
½ tbsp. yellow mustard seed
2 sticks cinnamon
½ tbsp. black peppercorns
¾ tbsp. whole cloves
¾ tbsp. whole allspice
1-inch piece fresh ginger
⅛ tsp. cayenne

Combine vegetables with salt in a large bowl and pour over hot water to cover. Let stand 12 hours. Drain and squeeze dry in a clean kitchen towel. Mix vinegar and sugar in a large kettle, add spices in spice bag and bring to a boil. Add vegetables, return to boil and boil gently for 30 minutes. Discard spice bag. Pack hot into hot, sterile pint jars, leaving ½ inch of head space. Pour over hot pickling liquid, again leaving ½ inch of head space. Seal and process 5 minutes in a boiling water bath.
—*Adapted from the NCHFP website*

❦ Picnic Relish

July 1910

Take large cucumbers, wash, pare, split, scrape out the seeds, and chop to equal 3 qts. Add 3 c. each of red and green bell peppers, chopped, and 1 c. chopped onion in large bowl. Use ¾ c. canning or pickling salt, mixing with vegetables, cover with ice and let stand in refrigerator for 4 hours. Drain, cover with ice again and let stand 1 more hour. Combine ½ tsp. cayenne pepper, 4 tsp. each of mustard seed, turmeric, whole allspice, and whole cloves in a spice bag and add to 6 c. cider vinegar at 5 percent acidity and 2 c. brown sugar. Bring to a boil, pour over vegetables, cover, and let stand in refrigerator 24 hours. Heat mixture to a boil, pack hot into hot, clean half-pint or pint jars, leaving ½ inch of head space, seal, and process 10 minutes in a boiling water bath.
—*Adapted from the NCHFP website*

❦ Bordeaux Relish

June 1917
This is a good relish for cold meats.

1 qt. green tomatoes
3 onions
2 qt. cabbage
1 red pepper
1 qt. 5 percent vinegar
½ tsp. allspice
¾ tbsp. brown mustard seeds
1 c. brown sugar
2 tbsp. canning or pickling salt

Wash and chop tomatoes, onions, cabbage, and red pepper to uniform fineness. Mix and add remaining ingredients. Boil for ½ hour. Pack hot into hot, sterilized half-pint or pint jars. Seal and store immediately in refrigerator.

HOW I CAN MY GARDEN AND ORCHARD
This is the Way Farm Women Preserve Food

June 1923

To can a garden and orchard successfully, much depends on the plans made before products are ripe or even planted.

I plan to plant good canning varieties. Green beans are better than wax. Some varieties of beets "bleed" worse than others; some sweet corn is never very sweet. The finished product cannot be better than the original.

It is better to have 50 cans of 5 varieties than the same amount of 1 kind. Last year, I had 41 kinds of finished products. I always can a few things my family claims they do not care for and when "winter comes," they welcome the variety.

After all these plans are made, the actual canning has to be done. Experience helps but a careful beginner can be about as successful as an experienced person by attention to detail. As a Girls' Food Club leader, I have found that girls' canned products are often superior to their mothers' *because they carry out instructions accurately*.

I have found it very important to keep records, including the name of variety, method used, amount of sugar, and estimate of cost. This record is a valuable guide the next year. I always try to make each can the best and last fall when I saw the premium tags on my products at our state fair and received a check for 50 dollars, I knew that in some cases, at least, I had succeeded.

—Mrs. B. G., Ohio

 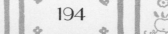

Chutneys

The farmer's wife relied on chutneys and other sauces to add spice to otherwise bland foods. All of the recipes in this section came first from *The Farmer's Wife Magazine* and have been adapted (except for refrigerator chutneys) from the NCHFP website and the Clemson University Extension Service website.

■■■

❧ Indian Chutney
September 1918

This recipe, completely lacking in spice, reflects the farmer's wife's preference for milder foods. You may add 1 tsp. ground ginger and ¼ c. whole mixed pickling spice in a spice bag at the initial boiling stage if you prefer a chutney that is somewhat peppier.

6 lbs. ripe tomatoes, washed, skinned, and chopped (to equal 3 qt.)
5 lbs. sour apples, peeled, cored, and chopped (to equal 3 qt.)
2 c. seedless raisins
2 c. onion, chopped
1 c. mixed green and red bell peppers, chopped
2 lbs. brown sugar
4 c. vinegar at 5 percent acidity
4 tsp. canning or pickling salt

Combine ingredients in a large pot and bring to a boil. Lower heat to boil gently for 1 hour, stirring frequently, til mixture is thick and reduced by one-half. Pack hot into hot, clean pint jars, leaving ½ inch of head space. Remove air bubbles, seal, and process 10 minutes in a boiling water bath.
—*Adapted from the NCHFP website*

❦ Apple Indian Chutney

September 1935

This is a hot, delicious sauce.

6 lbs. sour apples, peeled,
   cored, and chopped fine
2 lemons, chopped fine, peel
   and all, seeds removed
2 c. raisins, chopped fine
2 hot green peppers
1 large onion, chopped
2 lbs. brown sugar
1 tbsp. yellow mustard seed
1 tbsp. ground ginger
½ tbsp. canning or
   pickling salt
3 c. vinegar at 5 percent acidity

Mix apple with lemon to keep from turning dark. Remove seeds
from peppers and chop. Combine all ingredients. Bring to a boil
and cook slowly til apples are tender. Pack hot in hot, sterile pint
jars, seal, and store immediately in refrigerator.

❧ Green Gooseberry Chutney
June 1914

2 pt. green gooseberries
1½ c. seedless raisins
5 cloves garlic
¼ c. ground mustard
¼ c. ground ginger
10 tbsp. sugar
6 tbsp. canning or pickling salt
2 pt. 5 percent vinegar

Chop gooseberries, raisins, and garlic almost to a paste. Mix with remaining ingredients and boil for 45 minutes. Pack hot in hot, sterile pint jars. Seal and store immediately in refrigerator.

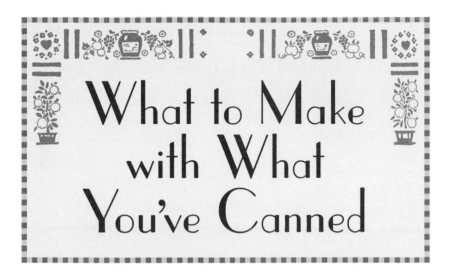

What to Make with What You've Canned

The *Farmer's Wife* had ideas aplenty on this topic and shelf upon shelf of preserved foods with which to experiment. The selection here is sure to appeal to today's taste buds.

Tomatoes

Scalloped Tomatoes
April 1910

Put a layer of canned tomato *(Editor's note: Use 1-quart jar of Whole Tomatoes Packed in Water from page 122.)* in a well-buttered baking dish. Season with salt and pepper, sprinkle over it 1 tsp. sugar, then add a layer of breadcrumbs, another of tomato, seasoning as before, and so on until the tomato is all used, having the top layer of bread over which put dots of butter. Bake at 375°F for at least an hour, letting the top get well browned.

If you happen to have a quantity of dried bread on hand (every scrap of bread should be saved and dried for such purposes), it may always be used for scalloping vegetables by soaking it first in cold water until soft; then squeeze out and use as directed above.

❦ Tomato Custard with Cheese Sauce
February 1934

1 qt. canned Whole Tomatoes Packed in Water (page 122)
1 tbsp. minced onion
1 tsp. salt
sprinkle of paprika
⅓ c. fine breadcrumbs
3 eggs, slightly beaten

Heat tomatoes, add onion, and put through sieve *[Editor's note: or run through blender til smooth]*. Add salt, paprika, crumbs, and eggs. Pour into buttered custard cups and bake at 350°F until firm. Serve with:

Cheese Sauce
1 tbsp. butter
1 tbsp. flour
¼ tsp. salt
¼ tsp. dry mustard
1 c. scalded milk
½ c. grated cheddar cheese

Melt butter and blend in flour and seasonings. Add milk and cook until thickened. Add cheese and pour over custards to serve.
—Mrs. M. R., New York

❦ Dixie Tomatoes
July 1911

1 qt. canned Whole Tomatoes Packed in Water (page 122)
3 finely chopped green peppers
2 tbsp. butter
salt and pepper to taste

Cook tomatoes and peppers together til tender, add butter, salt, and pepper and serve.

❦ Tomato Soup

August 1910

medium onion
small carrot
2 tbsp. butter
1 qt. canned Whole Tomatoes
     Packed in Water (page 122)
1 pt. beef broth
½ c. sweet cream or milk
salt and pepper to taste

Chop fine the onion and carrot. Fry in butter til quite soft and beginning to brown. Add canned tomatoes and beef broth. Simmer ½ hour then puree in blender or food processor. Return to fire with sweet cream or milk and warm through; season with salt and pepper to taste.

❦ Baked Onions and Tomatoes

Arrange small whole onions or sliced large ones in a baking dish. Season well with salt and pepper. Add enough canned tomatoes to just cover (page 122). Bake until onions are tender and liquid is nearly absorbed. Sprinkle with grated cheese.

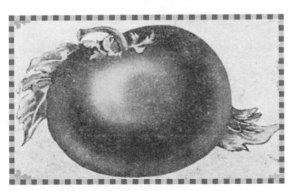

Carrots and Peas

❧ Harvard Carrots

½ c. sugar
½ tbsp. cornstarch
½ c. vinegar
1 pt. canned carrots
2 tbsp. butter

Mix sugar and cornstarch, add vinegar, and boil well. Pour over carrots and heat thoroughly. Add butter and serve.

❧ Creamed Peas
July 1911

1 tbsp. butter
1 tbsp. flour
1½ c. milk
few drops onion juice
½ tsp. sugar
1 qt. canned green peas, drained and rinsed

To make white sauce, melt butter and add flour and then milk, stirring til smooth. Add several drops of juice squeezed from an onion (sliced in half) and sugar. Add peas and let stand over hot water in double boiler til peas are heated through.

❦ Cream of Pea Soup
March 1918

The housewife whose shelves are supplied with [canned] vegetables has first-class material for nourishing, delicious, and inexpensive soups.

1 pt. canned peas
1 pt. cold water

White Sauce
8 tbsp. butter
4 tbsp flour
4 c. scalded milk
1 tsp. salt

Melt butter, add flour, and then add scalded milk and salt. Stir til smooth. Cook peas until soft and drain, reserving cooking water. Press peas through a coarse strainer and add cooking water. Combine peas with white sauce and heat through. Do not let the soup stand long before serving as it is likely to thicken too much. Serve very hot with crackers or bread cut in ½ inch cubes and toasted a delicate brown. To make a richer soup, add an egg, lightly beaten, or add a few teaspoonfuls of whipped cream to the soup just before serving.

Corn

❦ Savory Scalloped Corn

This is an excellent dish with fish.

2 c. canned tomatoes (page 122)
2 c. canned corn (page 144)
½ c. bread crumbs
salt and pepper to taste
3 tbsp. butter

Chop the tomato fine, or used chopped Tomatoes Packed in Water (page 122). Spread a cup of corn in the bottom of a well-greased baking dish, cover this with a cup of tomato, then sprinkle this with half the bread crumbs, season with salt and pepper, and dot over with butter. Repeat this layer and bake in a moderate oven 350°F for 20 minutes.

❦ Cream of Corn Soup

October 1910

1 qt. canned corn
3 pts. cold water
1 small slice onion, optional
salt and pepper to taste
1 c. sweet cream
or
1 c. thin white sauce (as for Cream of Pea Soup, page 203)

To each quart of canned corn add 3 pt. water and sliced onion, if desired. Boil til tender. Add 2 tbsp. butter and 1 tbsp. flour. Season to taste with salt and pepper and allow to boil up. Add 1 c. sweet cream or thin white sauce just before serving; allow to warm through but not to boil.

Variations: Replace corn with celery, turnip, potato, or bean to make other cream soups.

■■■

❧ Corn Chowder

2-inch cube salt pork
1 sliced onion
4 potatoes, peeled and cut into ½ inch cubes
1 qt. milk
1 pt. canned corn
salt and pepper to taste
8 crackers, moistened with milk

Fry out the fat from salt pork in a large skillet over medium-high heat.
Remove pork and discard, leaving drippings. Add the onion and cook
in drippings until brown. Add the potatoes and boiling water to cover.
Cook until the potatoes are soft, then add the milk and corn. Heat
to the boiling point, season, moisten the crackers with cold milk, and
serve them with the chowder.

■■■

❧ Corn Fritters
November 1912

1 c. canned corn, drained
2 c. flour
pinch salt
1 tbsp. sugar
1½ tsp. baking powder
½ c. to 1 c. water, enough to make a thick batter
enough lard to half fill a deep skillet
maple syrup or homemade sugar syrup

Mix first 5 ingredients together. Heat lard in a deep skillet til very hot.
Drop batter by spoonfuls into fat and allow to brown on one side.
Flip and brown on the second side. Remove to paper towels to drain.
Serve with maple syrup or homemade sugar syrup.

EMERGENCY MEALS FROM THE EMERGENCY SHELF

By Ina B. Rowe
April 1929

Many a printed page is devoted to that "Five-Foot Shelf" of books at which one need spend fifteen minutes a day in order to become a shining social success. I like to think of every kitchen, too, as having its five-foot shelf, to which a housewife may turn fifteen minutes before a meal is to be served, and find upon it "the makin's" of any course, from soup to dessert.

Though the bookshelf should be so close at hand as to invite constant use, the emergency food shelf is most useful when just out of reach. Otherwise one is tempted to squander its contents and leave nothing for those occasions that demand quick thinking and prompt action.

❦ Corn Pudding
November 1912

1 pt. canned corn, drained
2 tbsp. sugar
2 eggs
piece of butter the size of a walnut
1 c. milk

Put corn into a chopping bowl and chop very fine. Beat together sugar, eggs, butter, and milk. Add corn, pour into buttered baking dish, and bake at 350°F for 1 hour.

❧ Corn Soufflé
March 1939

2 tbsp. butter
2 tbsp. flour
½ c. milk
1 tsp. salt
½ tsp. paprika
1 pt. canned cream-style corn
3 eggs, separated

Melt butter, add flour, and blend. Add milk and cook until thick, stirring constantly. Add seasonings, corn, and egg yolks, then fold in stiffly beaten egg whites. Pour into buttered casserole and bake at 375°F for about 45 minutes.

❧ Corn Scramble
May 1926

¼ lb. bacon
6 eggs
1 pt. canned corn, drained
1 c. milk
salt and pepper

Fry bacon and cut in pieces. Leave in pan with about 2 tbsp. of fat. Beat eggs slightly, add milk and corn, and cook over low heat til thick and creamy, stirring all the time. Add salt and pepper to taste. Serve on toast or boiled noodles.

CANNING FOR COMPANY MEALS

July 1938

When asked how she managed home entertaining in her busy household, a farm woman in Virginia had several suggestions. She [said], "I do love company but must squeeze parties into a busy schedule, as we have three small children. Planning ahead is a big help.

"During canning season, I keep company needs in mind and make up what I call my company shelf. As far as quality goes, it is much the same as for the family, but these are a little extra special. Those two dozen jelly glasses that unmold so nicely are kept back and gradually filled with a variety of flavors, from batches that seem the nicest. I can some corn 'niblet' style, some graded peas, some matched halves of fruit poached in extra heavy syrup. This year I added cinnamon drop apples."

Try some of these ideas for your company shelf—slightly different cuts and packs of vegetables and fruits, with suggestions for how to use them in attractive ways.

Asparagus: whole stalks to serve hot with brown buttered crumbs or Hollandaise sauce; or chilled as salad with Russian dressing

Spinach or other greens: for soufflé or individual timbales

Beets: small ones, whole or sliced and lightly pickled for a garnish, relish, or in salad

Green beans: tender young whole beans for a hot vegetable or salad; combined with yellow wax beans, both diagonal cut

Corn: tender young corn, cream-style, for corn pudding

Some unusual vegetables to can: baby lima beans, Swiss chard stems, whole tomatoes canned in juice, corn on the cob, sliced summer squash, okra and tomatoes, whole baby carrots, celery root

Peach, apricot, or pear halves: stuffed with cheese, plain or jellied for salad; center filled with berries for fruit cup or fruit plate; for tarts, for fruit compote

Whole pears: in cinnamon or grenadine syrup for salad or meat garnish; plain for dessert sauce

Whole peaches or plums: plain for dessert sauce or in a fruit compote

Apples: whole or halves as cinnamon apples for meat garnish or salad; baked apples for dessert; sliced or quarter sections in heavy syrup for compote, or with quince for sauce, tarts, or upside down cake

Fruit mixture: for fruit cup, for plain jellied or frozen desserts or salads

Whole berries or pitted cherries: for fruit cup; as a garnish for salads; for shortcake, upside down cake, lattice-top pies or tarts; jellied for dessert or salad; in Bavarian cream or ice cream, on sundaes

Tomato juice: cocktail; breakfast fruit; for jellied tomato aspic; for clear and cream soups

Tomato sauce: for meats, fish, salad dressings

Other Vegetables

▪▪▪

❦ Spring Beans with Sour Sauce
February 1934

1 pt. canned string beans
2 shallots, minced
1½ tbsp. butter
½ c. sugar
½ c. vinegar
½ tsp. salt
pepper to taste

Heat beans and cook until fork tender; drain and keep warm. Cook shallots in butter until translucent and add sugar and melt all together. Add vinegar and seasoning, stirring constantly. Pour over beans.

▪▪▪

❦ Fried Asparagus
May 1911

Drain a can of asparagus and boil until tender. Drain. Make a loose batter the consistency of cream from 1 c. milk, 1 egg, and about ½ c. flour. Dip each asparagus stalk in batter and fry in hot butter or oil til lightly browned, drain well, sprinkle with salt, and serve hot.

▪▪▪

❦ Pumpkin Waffles
November 1912

1 c. canned pumpkin, drained
½ c. sugar
1 tsp. cinnamon

1 egg, beaten
1 c. milk
½ yeast cake, dissolved in ½ c. lukewarm water
2 tbsp. butter, melted
1 lb. sifted flour
sweet milk, to thin batter
pinch ginger

To each cupful of drained canned pumpkin, mashed and seasoned with sugar and cinnamon, add egg, milk, yeast cake dissolved in water, butter, and flour. Thin to rather a thick batter with sweet milk, allow to rise until light, about ½ hour, then beat in a pinch of ginger. Let this rise a second time for 20 minutes in a warm place and bake in a hot greased waffle iron. Have a warm plate with equal parts of fine sugar cinnamon mixed, butter the waffle, dip it in the cinnamon sugar, and serve immediately.

❦ Red Dressing for Head Lettuce
November 1924

1 tbsp. chili sauce
5 tbsp. olive oil
2 tbsp. vinegar
salt, pepper, and paprika, to taste
sprinkle dry mustard

Blend all thoroughly then add:

½ tbsp. hard-cooked egg yolk, chopped
½ tbsp. hard-cooked egg white, chopped
½ tbsp. shallot, minced and browned in a little olive oil
½ tbsp. chives or parsley, chopped

Mix all together and serve on lettuce salad.

THERE'S BOTH RHYME AND REASON IN AUNT MARTHA'S USES FOR PICKLE JUICES

The last time I was at Aunt Martha's she said, rather apologetically, as she cut her mince pie, "My mincemeat wasn't as good as usual this year. I didn't have any fruit pickle juice handy. And do you know, I saw one hostess, when our club met, pour that lovely, rich syrup from her peach pickles down the sink! I was simply flabbergasted!"

When Aunt Martha uses that word to describe some person's actions or sayings, I know it must be a terrible crime. So I asked her how she used her pickle juice besides in mincemeat, and she gave me many ideas.

When you stop to think of it, there are many uses for that combination: good vinegar, sugar, and spices. And fruit pickles have a characteristic fruit flavor that makes them especially choice. I hope your pickle juice is not so highly spiced or darkened by free spice that its use is limited to mincemeat.

Harvard Beets

Melt 2 tbsp. butter, add 2 level tbsp. flour and ½ c. sweet pickle juice. Cook until thick. Pour over and let stand on hot cooked and diced beets for a 1 pt. jar until they absorb the flavor of the sauce.

Fruit Salad Dressing

Mix together 1½ level tbsp. flour, ½ tsp. mustard, ½ tsp. salt, and about 1 tbsp. sugar. Beat with 2 eggs or 4 yolks, add 1 c. rich pickle juice, and cook in a double boiler or heavy saucepan, stirring constantly, until thick. Remove and cool. To use, fold in about an equal amount of fluffy whipped cream. This is especially good with banana or apple salads or carrot and cabbage salad mixed with fruit or nuts.

❦ Sour Cream Dressing

Mix in a double boiler or heavy saucepan 1 c. thick sour cream, ½ c. sweet pickle juice, 2 whole eggs or 4 yolks (beaten first), and salt as needed. Heat to boiling and stir until thick. Cool and use.

Other uses:
- As a spicy syrup in which to cook apples and to serve with meat
- To moisten sandwich spreads, as peanut butter
- As a basis for a sweet French dressing (pickle juice, oil or cream, a little seasoning)

Fruits

❦ Cheese and Marmalade Sandwiches
June 1914

To 1 c. cottage cheese add salt to season and ½ c. orange marmalade. Mix to a smooth paste. Spread on thin slices of buttered bread or on unsweetened crackers and make into sandwiches.

❦ Baked Gingered Pears
January 1929

Spread canned pears with syrup from a jar of preserved ginger. Sprinkle with lemon juice and stick a clove in each pear piece. Place in casserole and bake at 350°F until heated through, or preferably, til well-browned. Serve hot, with a roast.

❦ Rhubarb Brown Betty from Canned Rhubarb
April 1925

2 c. fine breadcrumbs
3 c. canned, sweetened rhubarb (from Other Preserved Fruits
    and Fruit Product chapter, page 108)
pie spice to taste
¼ c. unsalted butter
⅓ c. brown sugar heavy cream to serve

Cover bottom of 9-inch baking pan with a thick layer of breadcrumbs.
Cover crumbs with layer of rhubarb, sprinkle with spice, and dot
with butter. Place another layer of crumbs over this and cover
with rhubarb as before. Cover with another layer of crumbs. Pour
melted butter over the crumbs which form top layer, sprinkle with
brown sugar, and bake at 350°F for 45 minutes. Serve with plain or
whipped cream.

❦ Cherry Turnovers
June 1910

1 c. butter
1 lb. flour
1 c. or less ice water
1 qt. jar cherries in syrup, drained
2 eggs, well beaten
lemon juice
confectioner's sugar, for sprinkling

Rub butter into flour; when like coarse meal, moisten with ice water and work to a paste, handling as little as possible. Roll out on a floured board, fold up, and roll for the second and third time, if still very cold, use at once, if not, set in the ice box until chilled. Roll out and cut into rounds the size of large biscuits. Drain juice off sweetened canned cherries and chop; mix with eggs, and several drops lemon juice. Place 1 tbsp. of the cherry mixture on each round of the crust, fold in half, and pinch edges together. Lay these half-circles on a floured or buttered tin and bake to a golden brown at 375°F. Sift sugar over them and serve either hot or cold.

❦ Cherry Bread Pudding
June 1910

2 pts. canned cherries packed in water or very light syrup
loaf of stale bread
3 eggs
1 pt. milk
¾ c. sugar
cream and sugar to serve

Drain the juice from a can of stoned cherries, reserving the juice and chopping the cherries slightly. Cut the crust from a loaf of stale bread and discard, slice bread thin, spread the slices with cherries, pack in a deep buttered dish, and pour the cherry juice over all. Set aside until the juice is all absorbed by the bread. Make a custard of the eggs, milk, and sugar. Pour this over the bread. If it does not quite cover the bread, add more milk. Cover and bake at 350°F until custard is set. Serve with cream and sugar.

CHERRY PIE 3 WAYS FROM CANNED CHERRIES

May 1938

❦ Crust

1 ½ c. flour
½ tsp. salt
⅔ c. lard
¼ c. ice water

Sift flour once before measuring, then sift with salt. Distribute lard by spoonfuls around flour; mix quickly. Add water a little at a time, until moist enough that dough will just hold together. Gather quickly with 1 hand and roll together.
—*Eleanor Enos, Ohio*

❦ Indiana Cherry Pie

3 tbsp. cornstarch
½ c. juice from canned cherries packed in light syrup
1 c. sugar
1 tbsp. unsalted butter
pinch salt
3 c. unsweetened canned cherries (water-packed)

Mix cornstarch and cherry juice in double boiler til thick, stirring constantly. Add sugar and cook 5 minutes longer. Remove from heat, add butter, salt, and cherries, stirring carefully. Let stand. Roll out crust and spread in dish. Pour in cherry mixture, cover with top crust, and cut to allow for escape of steam. Seal edges, bake 15 minutes at 425°F, then 30 minutes at 350°F.
—*Mary Wien, Indiana*

❧ Ohio Cherry Pie

2 tbsp. flour, divided
3 c. drained, unsweetened canned cherries (water packed)
¼ c. juice from canned cherries packed in light syrup
1¼ c. sugar, divided
sprinkle salt
2 tbsp. milk

Line pan with pastry. Sprinkle with 1 tbsp. flour. Wet around rim edge. Spread with half the cherries. Mix well together 1 c. sugar, salt, and remaining 1 tbsp. flour. Sprinkle half sugar mixture over top of cherries. Cover with remaining cherries and juice and sprinkle rest of sugar mixture on top. Put on upper crust, brush top with milk, and sprinkle lightly with ¼ c. sugar. Bake at 425°F, about 45 minutes.
—*Eleanor Enos, Ohio*

❧ Michigan Cherry Pie

3 c. cherries, canned without sugar, drained (water packed)
1 c. juice from canned cherries packed in light syrup
1¼ c. sugar
3½ tbsp. cornstarch
2 tbsp. unsalted butter
½ tsp. almond extract

Mix cherries, juice, and sugar. Allow to stand 15 minutes or longer while crust is being made. Drain juice from cherries. Mix cornstarch with a little of the juice until smooth. Bring remaining juice to a boil; stir in cornstarch mixture. Boil, stirring constantly, for 1 minute. Remove from flame, add butter. Let cool until crust is rolled out. Add cherries and extract to thickened juice; pour into crust. Adjust top crust; press down edges with a fork. Cut off excess pastry. Bake at 425°F until crust is golden brown, about 45 minutes.
—*Annabel Jones, Michigan*

❦ Fried Canned Peaches
January 1926

Drain a can of peaches packed in water or light syrup. Sprinkle with sugar and fry 1 minute on each side in melted butter. Serve with hot syrup which forms in pan from sugar, butter, and juice.

Variation: Pears may be cooked in same way.

❦ Poached Pears
January 1926

1 can pears, packed in juice
sugar
plain cake (such as pound cake)

Drain pears and measure juice. Add equal amount sugar as juice and stir over fire to dissolve. Cook pears carefully in syrup 2 minutes then place on cake slices when ready to serve. Serve with hot syrup. For a special dessert, rounds of ice cream may be placed on cake under pears.

Variation: Peaches may be used.

❦ Plum Pie

September 1920

Editor's note: A recipe using not a canned product from the store, but plum pulp left over from jelly making.

2 c. sugar
2 tbsp. flour
1 tsp. cinnamon
2 c. plum pulp from jelly making
2 sheets commercial puff pastry, for 2 pies

Mix sugar, flour, and cinnamon, then stir in pulp. Line pastry tins with slightly thawed puff pastry rolled thin, then fill with plum mixture. Bake at 350°F til lightly golden.

❦ Currant Punch

August 1928

2 c. boiling water
1 glass currant jelly
½ c. sugar
3 tbsp. lemon juice

Pour the boiling water over jelly and let stand until jelly is thoroughly dissolved. Add sugar and lemon juice and chill. Just before serving dilute with ice and water to taste.

Variation: There is almost no limit to the variety of delicious drinks that can be made with . . . melted jellies, combined with lemon juice and the grated lemon rind to give zest. If lemon is lacking, orange juice, rhubarb juice, or vinegar may be substituted to give the required acid, but lemon juice not only has a distinctive flavor of its own, it helps to emphasize the distinctive flavors of all the fruits put with it.

Additional Resources for Information about Canning and Pickling

The science of preserving is ever-changing, with experts at federally funded university extension services testing and making updates to existing recommendations on a regular basis. There is, therefore, an abundance of information available to the home canner. To find the extension service for your area, visit **www.csrees.usda.gov/Extension/**

Additionally, your local extension service will have information on preserving products native to your area—wild fruits, for example—and may also be testing updates for products similar to those that are now recommended in this book for refrigeration only. They can answer any questions you have about methods and safety, such as how to test a pressure canner, how to make adjustments for altitude, and how to dispose of food that is potentially contaminated.

The USDA's National Center for Home Food Preservation
is another excellent resource:
www.uga.edu/nchfp/publications/publications_usda.html
*(This link allows you to download and print the USDA's
"Complete Guide to Home Canning.")*

The University of Georgia's (UGA) cooperative extension service
for food preservation is a helpful site as well:
www.fcs.uga.edu/ext/pubs/food/canning.php

Additionally, the UGA's "So Easy to Preserve"—a print version
with more than 185 tested recipes that includes the USDA's latest
recommendations, as well as a series of demonstration DVDs,
are available from **www.uga.edu/setp/**

Other sources consulted for this book:
The Clemson University Extension Service Food Safety &
Preservation website (**http://hgic.clemson.edu/food.htm**), and
the University of Minnesota Cooperative Extension Service website
(**http://www.extension.umn.edu/distribution/nutrition/
DJ1089.html**)